Structured Query Language (SQL)

A Practical Introduction

STRUCTURED QUERY LANGUAGE (SQL)

A Practical Introduction

AKEEL I DIN

First published 1994

Editorial office: NCC Blackwell Ltd., Oxford House, Oxford Road, Manchester M1 7ED, UK.

NCC Blackwell Ltd.
108 Cowley Road
Oxford OX4 1JF
UK

Blackwell Publishers
238 Main Street
Cambridge, Massachusetts 02142
USA

British Library Cataloguing in Publication Data

British Library data is available.

American Library of Congress Data

Library of Congress data is available.

Typeset in 11.5 on 13pt Times by H & H Graphics, Blackburn.
Printed in Great Britain by Hartnolls Ltd., Bodmin, Cornwall.

ISBN 1–85554–357–5

This book is printed on acid-free paper.

Contents

To my loving parents,
Dr M Q and Mrs R B Din

1

Introduction

The Structured Query Language, SQL is a query language which is used with relational databases. This chapter starts by describing some of the terms used in data processing and how they relate to SQL. The latter part of this chapter describes relational databases and how SQL is used to query them.

1.1 A Collection of Related Data: Databases and Database Management Systems

Let's start from basics. What is a database? In very general terms, a database is a collection of related data. Notice the word related, this implies that the collection of letters on this page do not by themselves constitute a database. But if we think of them as a collection of letters arranged to form words, then they can be conceptualised as data in a database. Using similar reasoning, we can also say that a tome such as a telephone directory is also a database. It is a database first, because it is a collection of letters that form words and second, because it is an alphabetical listing of people's names, their addresses and their telephone numbers. How we think of a database depends on what use we want to make of the information that it contains.

So far, we have talked about a database in its broadest sense. This very general definition is not what most people mean when they talk about a database. In this electronic age, the word database has become synonymous with the term "computerised database". Collins English Dictionary describes a database as 'a store of a large amount of information, especially in a form that can be handled by a computer'. In this book, we will be dealing only with computerised databases. In keeping with popular trend though, we will be using the word database to refer to a computerised database.

A database (computerised database remember) by itself, is not much use. The data is stored electronically on the computer's disk in a format which we humans cannot read or understand directly. What we need is some way of accessing this data and converting it into a form which we do understand.

1

This is the job of the database management system or DBMS for short. A DBMS is essentially a suite of programs that act as the interface between the human operator and the data held in the database. Using the DBMS, it is possible to retrieve useful information, update or delete obsolete information and add new information to the database. As well as data entry and retrieval, the DBMS plays an important role in maintaining the overall integrity of the data in the database. The simplest example is of ensuring that the values entered into the database conform to the data types that are specified. For example, in the telephone book database, the DBMS might have to ensure that each phone number entered conforms to a set format of XXX-XXXXXXX where X represents an integer.

1.2   The Database as a Collection of Tables: Relational databases and SQL

In the early days of computerised databases, all large database systems conformed to either the network data model or the hierarchical data model. We will not be discussing the technical details of these models except to say that they are quite complex and not very flexible. One of the main drawbacks of these databases was that in order to retrieve information, the user had to have an idea of where in the database the data was stored. This meant that data processing and information retrieval was a technical job which was beyond the ability of the average office manager. In those days life was simple. data processing staff were expected to prepared the annual or monthly or weekly reports and managers were expected to formulate and implement day to day business strategy according to the information contained in the reports. Computer literate executives were rare and DP staff with business sense were even more rare. This was the state of affairs before the advent of relational databases.

The relational data model was introduced in 1970, E. F. Codd, a research fellow working for IBM, in his article *'A Relational Model of Data for Large Shared Databanks'*. The relational database model represented the database as a collection of tables which related to one another.

Unlike network and hierarchical databases, the relational database is quite intuitive to use, with data organised into tables, columns and rows. An example of a relational database table is shown in Figure 1.1. We can see just by looking at Figure 1.1 what this table is. The table is a list of names and telephone numbers. It is similar to how we might go about the task of jotting down the phone numbers of some of our friends, in the back of our diary for example.

NUM	SURNAME	FIRSTNAME	PHONE_NUMBER
1	Jones	Frank	9635
2	Bates	Norman	8313
3	Clark	Brian	2917
4	Stonehouse	Mark	3692
5	Warwick	Rita	3487

Figure 1.1   A relational database table

The relational data model consists of a number of intuitive concepts for storing any type of data in a database, along with a number of functions to manipulate the information. The relational data model as proposed by Codd provided the basic concepts for a new database management system, the relational database management system (RDBMS). Soon after the relational model was defined, several relational database languages were developed and used for instructing the RDBMS. Structured Query Language being one of them.

The SQL language is so inextricably tied to relational database theory that it is impossible to discuss it without also discussing the relational data model. The next two sections briefly describe some of the concepts of this model.

1.2.1 Tables, columns and rows

We have already seen that a relational database stores data in tables. Each column of the table represent an attribute, SURNAME, FIRSTNAME, PHONE_NUMBER for example. Each row in the table is a record. In the

NUM	D-O-B	DEPT	GRADE
2	12/10/63	ENG	4
5	07/05/50	DESIGN	7
3	03/11/45	SALES	9
1	09/03/73	ENG	2

Figure 1.2   Additional details table

table in Figure 1.1, each row is a record of one person. A single table with a column and row structure, does not represent a relational database. Technically, this is known as a flat file or card index type database. Relational databases have several tables with interrelating data. Suppose that the information in the table of Figure 1.1 is actually the list of people working in a company with their telephone extensions. Now we get an idea that this simple table is actually a small part of the overall database, the personnel database. Another table, such as the one in Figure 1.2. could contain additional details on the persons listed in the first table.

1.2.2   The Primary key and the foreign Key

The two tables described in the previous section and shown in Figures 1.1 and 1.2, now constitute a relational database. Of course, in a real personnel database, you would need to store a great deal more information and would thus need a lot more related tables.

Notice that the first column in each table is the NUM column. The information stored in NUM does not really have anything to do with the person's record. Why is it there? The reason is that NUM is used to uniquely identify each person's record. We could have used the person's name, but chances are that in a large company, there would be more than one person with the same name. NUM is known as the primary key for the table of Figure 1.1. For the table of Figure 1.2, where a primary key of another table is used to relate data, NUM is a called a foreign key.

The primary keys and foreign keys are a very important part of relational databases. They are the fields that relate tables to each other. In the table of Figure 1.2 for example, we know that the first record is for Norman Bates because the value for NUM is 2 and we can see from the table of Figure 1.1 that this is Norman Bates' record.

1.3   Communicating to the DBMS what you want it to do: Introduction to the SQL language.

The Structured Query Language is a relational database language. By itself, SQL does not make a DBMS. It is just a medium which is used as a means of communicating to the DBMS what you want it to do. SQL commands consist of 'English-like' statements which are used to query, insert, update and delete data. What we mean by 'English-like', is that SQL commands resemble English language sentences in their construction and use. This does not mean that you can type in something like "Pull up the figures for last quarter's sales" and expect SQL to understand your request. What it does mean is that SQL is a lot easier to learn and understand than most of the other computer languages.

SQL is sometimes referred to as a non-procedural database language. This means that when you issue an SQL command to retrieve data from a database, you do not have to explicitly tell SQL where to look for the data. It is enough just to tell SQL what data you want to be retrieved. The DBMS will take care of locating the information in the database. This is very useful because it means that users do not need to have any knowledge of where the data is and how to get at it. Procedural languages such as COBOL or Pascal and even older databases based on the network and hierarchical data models require that users specify what data to retrieve and also how to get at it. Most large corporate databases are held on several different computers in different parts of the building or even at different geographic locations. In such situations, the non-procedural nature of SQL makes flexible, ad hoc querying and data retrieval possible. Users can construct and execute an SQL query, look at the data retrieved, and change the query if needed all in a spontaneous manner. To perform similar queries using a procedural language such as COBOL would mean that you would have to create, compile and run one computer program for each query.

Commercial database management systems allow SQL to be used in two distinct ways. First, SQL commands can be typed at the command line directly. The DBMS interprets and processes the SQL commands immediately, and any result rows that are retrieved are displayed. This method of SQL processing is called interactive SQL. The second method is called programmatic SQL. Here, SQL statements are embedded in a host language such as COBOL or C. SQL needs a host language because SQL is not really a complete computer programming language as such. It has no statements or constructs that allow a program to branch or loop. The host language provides the necessary looping and branching structures and the interface with the user, while SQL provides the statements to communicate with the DBMS.

1.4 A Research Project Conducted by IBM: The history of SQL

The origins of the SQL language date back to a research project conducted by IBM at their research laboratories in San Jose, California in the early 1970s. The aim of the project was to develop an experimental RDBMS which would eventually lead to a marketable product. At that time, there was a lot of interest in the relational model for databases at the academic level, in conferences and seminars. IBM, which already had a large share of the commercial database market with hierarchical and network model DBMSs, realised quite quickly that the relational model would figure prominently in future database products.

The project at IBM's San Jose labs was started in 1974 and was named System R. A language called Sequel (for Structured English QUEry Language) was chosen as the relational database language for System R. In the project, Sequel was abbreviated to SQL. This is the reason why SQL is still generally pronounced as see-quel.

In the first phase of the System R project, researchers concentrated on developing a basic version of the RDBMS. The main aim at this stage was to verify that the theories of the relational model could be translated into a working, commercially viable product. This first phase was successfully completed by the end of 1975, and resulted in a rudimentary, single-user DBMS based on the relational model.

The subsequent phases of System R concentrated on further developing the DBMS from the first phase. Additional features were added, multi-user capability was implemented, and by 1978, a completed RDBMS was ready for user evaluation. The System R project was finally completed in 1979. During this time, the SQL language was modified and added to as the needs of the System R DBMS dictated.

The theoretical work of the System R project resulted in the development and release in 1981 of IBM's first commercial relational database management system. The product was called SQL/DS and ran under the DOS/VSE operating system environment. Two years later, IBM announced a version of SQL/DS for the VM/CMS operating system. In 1983, IBM released a second SQL based RDBMS called DB2, which ran under the MVS operating system. DB2 quickly gained widespread popularity and even today, versions of DB2 form the basis of many database systems found in large corporate data-centres.

During the development of System R and SQL/DS, other companies were also at work creating their own relational database management systems. Some of them, Oracle being a prime example, even implemented SQL as the relational database language for their DBMSs concurrently with IBM.

Today, the SQL language has gained ANSI (American National Standards Institute) and ISO (International Standards Organization) certification. A version of SQL is available for almost any hardware platform from CRAY supercomputers to IBM PC microcomputers. In recent years, there has been a marked trend for software manufacturers to move away from proprietary database languages and settle on the SQL standard. The microcomputer platform especially has seen a proliferation of previously proprietary packages that have implemented SQL functionality. Even spreadsheet and word processing packages have added options which allow data to be sent to and retrieved from SQL based databases via a Local Area or a Wide Area network connection.

1.5   SQL Commands Build Upon Themselves: Organization of this book

After this introduction, this book first presents the SQL language in a nutshell. Subsequent chapters then focus on explaining each of the SQL command groups (the SELECT, the UPDATE, the CREATE, etc) more fully. The reason for this method of presentation is that a lot of the SQL commands build upon themselves. For example, you cannot discuss the INSERT INTO with SELECT command without having knowledge of and understanding the SELECT statement itself. So where do you put the chapter on INSERT INTO with SELECT? You can't put it before the chapter on SELECT because as we've said, it requires the reader to have knowledge of the SELECT statement. You can't put it after the chapter on SELECT because the SELECT operates on data input into the tables by the INSERT statement. We have gone for the second option because it is a lot easier to take a leap of faith and believe that somehow the tables are already populated with data and use SELECT to query them rather than trying to understand the INSERT INTO with SELECT without any knowledge of how SELECT works.

To save having to put phrases such as "see the later chapter on SELECT" or "see the earlier chapter on INSERT" throughout the book, we have started off by describing the SQL language globally, and then detailing each command group separately. It's a bit like a course for auto mechanics, say, you start off by first describing the layout of the car and all its major parts such as the engine, the gearbox, etc, before going on to discuss topics like the detailed construction of the engine.

Primarily, this book is designed to teach you how to use SQL to create, modify, maintain and use databases in practical situations. It is not intended to be an academic treatise on the subject, and so does not go into the mathematical basis of the topics considered. What it does contain is lots of examples and discussions on how they work. You should work your way through this book by reading through a section, and actually trying out each SQL query presented for yourself. If you do not have access to an SQL based database, then you can order a fully functional ANSI/ISO SQL database at an affordable price, by sending off the order form at the back of this book. The quickest and easiest method of learning SQL (or indeed any computer language) is to use it in real life, practical situations. The chapters of this book are laid out so that each section builds upon the information and examples presented in the previous chapters. By following the SQL query examples, you will create a database, populate it and then use it to retrieve information.

Remember that the SQL queries in this book are only given as examples. They represent one possible method of retrieving the results that you want. As you gain confidence in SQL, you may be able to construct a more elegant query to solve a problem than the one that we have used. This just goes to show the power and flexibility of SQL.

The structure of this book is such that as you progress through it, you will be exposed to more and more complex aspects of SQL. If you follow through the book, you will find that you are not suddenly presented with anything particularly difficult. Rather, you will be gradually lead through and actively encouraged to try out SQL queries and variations of queries until you have thoroughly understood the underlying ideas.

The chapters will not all take the same amount of time to read and understand. You will benefit most if you sit down, start at a new section, and work your way through until it is completed. Although we understand that you may find some of the longer sections difficult to finish in one session. You should nonetheless endeavour to complete each section in as few sittings as possible. Taking short breaks to think over concepts learned as you progress through the section is also a good idea as it reinforces the learning process. You should try to understand the underlying concepts of what you are learning rather than coasting through the book.

1.5.1   Notational conventions

The following notational conventions are used throughout this book:

BOLD TYPE	These are keywords and data in a statement. They are to appear exactly as they are shown in bold.
{ }	Curly braces group together logically distinct sections of a command. If the braces are followed by an asterix (*), then the section inside them can occur zero or more times in a statement. If followed by a plus (+), then the section inside must appear at least once in the statement.

[   ]   Square brackets are used to signify sections of a statement that are optional.

(   )   Parentheses in bold are part of the SQL command, and must appear as shown. Parentheses which are not in bold are to indicate the logical order of evaluation.

. . .   The leader dots show that the section immediately proceeding them may be repeated any number of times.

| The vertical bar means 'or'.

Throughout this book, SQL command structure will be explained by using examples of actual statements.

2

A Rough Guide to SQL

This chapter presents an overview of the SQL language. The major commands are described from a functional point of view. Emphasis is given on briefly describing the SQL statements used in creating, populating, querying and modifying the database tables. It is left to the later chapters to give a detailed description of each command. This chapter gives you a feel for the SQL language and its main command groups.

2.1   Consider the Simple Address Book: A Basic Relational Database

As we have already seen, the relational database model represents the database as a collection of tables which relate to each other. Tables consist of rows and columns. The column definitions describe the fields in the table, while the rows are the data records in the table. For example, consider the simple address book. If we wanted to computerise this, we could represent it as a relational database table. The table would consist of columns and rows. For a typical address book, the table column headings might be SURNAME, FIRSTNAME, TELEPHONE, ADDRESS, RATING, as in Figure 2.1, where RATING is a measure of how close a friend the person is! Notice how the column headings for a table appear exactly as they would in a written version of the address book. The sequence in which the columns are defined when the table is first created is important to SQL. This will be most evident when we come to adding data using the INSERT command. The column names in a table must all be different but you can use numbers to distinguish between similar columns. For example NAME1 and NAME2 are valid column names. In practice though, this would be a poor choice because they do not describe the contents of the columns in any way. A much better choice would have been something like FIRSTNAME and INITIALS. The columns are a method of giving the table a structure in which to add our data records. You can think of a database table as a blank sheet of paper. In this case the overall objective is to use that sheet to store the names and addresses of people we know.

SQL Tips

> IBM's DB2 restricts user names to 8 characters but allows 18 characters in table and column names.

SURNAME	FIRSTNAME	TELEPHONE	ADDRESS	RATING
Jones	Andrew	(0523) 346639	267 The Firs LE4 6TY	15554
Mason	James	(0553) 786139	1933 Tripsom Close	12224
Malins	Dick	(0553) 867139	1966 Gt Glenn Rd	13444
McGinn	Mick	(0525) 567139	145 Glossop St	15664
Walsh	Paul	(0553) 656739	The Manor LE6 9PH	16778

Figure 2.1   Sample address book

The actual entries that you make into the table will form the rows (or records). So ('Jones', 'Andrew', '(0523) 346639' '767 The Firs LE4 6TY' 15554) is a valid record in the table of Figure 2.1. Note how the data in the record row is organised in the same sequence as the column headings in the table.

As we have defined it, the address book table is a pretty bad database. In order to understand what exactly is wrong with our table, we need to consider some 'what if' situations.

- What would happen if two or more people lived at the same address? We would need to have a separate entry for each friend, but with the same ADDRESS field contents.

- What if some of the people have more than one phone number? We would need to have a separate row in our table for each phone number.

These two 'what ifs' show that the current address book definition will lead to disorganised rows and a lot of redundant data (in the more than one phone number example, we would have two rows with exactly the same information except for the PHONE_NUMBER field).

Fortunately, the relational database model lets us create multiple related tables to form a database. When analyzing a real life problem (such as the address book problem), a formal method of resolving the tables' columns and their relationships can be used. This method, known as Data Normalization, was first suggested by Codd in 1972. Although it is beyond the scope of this

FRNO	SURNAME	FIRSTNAME	RATING
1	Jones	Andrew	15554
2	Mason	James	12224
3	Malins	Dick	13444
4	McGinn	Mick	15664
5	Walsh	Paul	16778

The NAMES Table

FRNO	ADDRESS
1	267 The Firs LE4 6TY
2	1933 Tripsom Close
3	1966 Gt Glenn Rd
4	145 Glossop St
5	The Manor LE6 9PH

The ADDRESS Table

FRNO	TELEPHONE
1	(0523) 346639
2	(0553) 786139
3	(0553) 867139
4	(0525) 567139
5	(0553) 656739

The TELEPHONE_ NUMBER Table

Figure 2.2 Data normalization

book to discuss Data Normalization fully, the contents of the next few paragraphs derive from this method.

Logically, we can split up the address book into three tables. The first table to hold details of who our friends are, the second to hold details of where they live, and the third table to hold details of phone numbers where they can be contacted. We don't really need a table for the ratings because a friend cannot have more than one rating at the same time. So we can add RATING to the NAMES table. If we wanted to keep a historical record of the ratings, however, then we would have to have a separate table for ratings as well.

Figure 2.2 shows how our address book can be split up to form a true relational database. Each table has a new field, FRNO. This field is the primary key in the NAMES table, and a foreign key in the other tables. It is what relates the tables to each other. A record which refers to a particular friend will have the same FRNO in all the tables. Thus, for our friend who has two houses, there will be an entry in tables one and three and two entries in table two.

In this simple example, the splitting up of the database into three tables is not very practical. For a personal address book, we would have been better off with the flat file (single table) database. The point to note though is that the three table version of the database is more flexible (we can store the details of a friend even if he has 25 telephones and 14 houses, without having to store redundant data). For large and complex databases which may consist of dozens of tables and tens of thousands of records, this logical splitting up of data into separate tables (known as Data Normalization) is vital in preventing data redundancy and creating a relationally correct database.

2.2 SQL Commands Fall into Different Categories: Subdivisions of SQL

The SQL language as defined by ANSI is subdivided into a number of different sections. This means that the SQL commands fall into different categories depending on what function they perform.

The Data Definition Language or DDL, (called Schema Definition Language by ANSI) consists of those commands in SQL that directly create database objects such as tables, indexes views. A lot of SQL commands also create temporary database objects during processing. The SELECT command for example, creates a temporary table to hold the results of a query. Such commands are not part of the DDL.

The Data Manipulation Language or DML consists of those commands which operate on the data in the database. This includes statements which add data to the tables as well as those statements which are used to query the database.

A third, unofficial, subdivision of SQL commands is Data Control Language or DCL. It is generally used to refer to those SQL commands that are used for data security. These are commands that are used to determine whether a user is allowed to carry out a particular operation or not. The ANSI standard groups these commands as being part of the DDL.

2.3 Enter SQL Statements at the Command Line: Using Interpretive SQL

All SQL statements in this book have been run using the Data-Lab SQL RDBMS and interpreter. The interpreter is the interface that you use to communicate with the DBMS. It allows you to type, compose and edit your SQL queries and has special editing commands to help you with this. When you are satisfied with the wording of the query, you can enter a semicolon character which instructs the interpreter to pass the query on to the SQL engine for processing.

If you are using a different SQL interpreter, you will in most cases, not need to modify the SQL statements because they follow the ANSI standard quite closely. Where extensions to the ANSI standard are discussed, you will need to consult the reference manual for your product to find out the exact form of the statement. Note that since Data-Lab SQL is quite close to Oracle SQL, Oracle users should have no problems.

2.4 Use the CREATE TABLE statement: Creating Database Tables

The SQL command to create tables is the CREATE TABLE statement. We will use this to create a simple car dealership database which will be used throughout the rest of this chapter. This simple database consists of the three tables shown in Figure 2.3. The CARS table holds details of the car's model name, the body style and the year of manufacturer. The MD_NUM field is used as the primary key. The SPECS table stores the information on additional equipment on each of the cars. The STOCK table holds details of the number of cars of each model that are currently in stock, and their retail price.

To create the first table in the car dealership database:

```
CREATE TABLE CARS (
    MD_NUM        INTEGER,
    MD-NAME       CHAR (10),
    STYLE         CHAR (6),
    YEAR          INTEGER ) ;
```

Table CARS created.

MD_NUM	MD_NAME	STYLE	YEAR

Cars table

MD_NUM	MPG	RADIO	ENGINE

Specs table

MD_NUM	QTY	PRICE

Stock table

Figure 2.3   Tables used in the used car dealership database

This statement creates a database table on disk, and assigns it the name CARS. The table's columns are also defined along with their data types. When you create tables, each of the columns must be defined as a specific data type. For example, the MD_NUM column is defined as an INTEGER, and MD_NAME is defined as CHAR(10). This means that when data is added to the table, the MD_NUM column will only hold integers and the MD_NAME column will hold character string values up to a maximum of 10 characters. The subject of data types and valid and invalid values will be discussed in detail in the next chapter.

Now that we have seen how to use the CREATE TABLE statement, we can create the next two tables in our car dealership database by typing:

```
CREATE TABLE SPECS  (
   MD_NUM        INTEGER,
   MD–NAME       INTEGER,
   RADIO         CHAR (3),
   ENGINE        CHAR (7)  ) ;
```

Table SPECS successfully created.

```
CREATE TABLE STOCK (
   MD_NUM        INTEGER,
   QTY           INTEGER,
   PRICE         INTEGER ) ;
```

When created, the tables are empty. In order to be of any use they need data. The next section describes the INSERT statement which is used to add data to the tables.

SQL Tips

Oracle allows you to use up to 30 characters for both table and column names.

2.5   Use the INSERT INTO Statement: Adding Data to Tables

Data is added to tables by using the INSERT statement. The values that we need to add to the car dealership database are shown in Figure 2.4.

Starting with the first table, the CARS table, the first record or row is added by:

```
INSERT INTO CARS (MS_NUM, MD_NAME, STYLE, YEAR)
VALUES  (1, 'HONDA', 'COUPE', 1983);
```

One row successfully inserted.

The rest of the rows can be added to CARS by using exactly the same statement format, but changing data values each time.

MD_NUM	MD_NAME	STYLE	YEAR
1	HONDA	COUPE	1983
2	TOYOTA	SALOON	1990
3	BUICK	ESTATE	1991
4	NISSAN	VAN	1992
5	FORD	SALOON	1993

The Cars Table

MD_NUM	MPG	RADIO	ENGINE
1	43	YES	2L-4CYL
2	25	NO	4L-V8
3	18	YES	5L-V8
4	50	NO	2L-4CYL
5	45	YES	3L-V6

The Specs Table

MD_NUM	QTY	PRICE
1	10	4980
2	3	13865
3	5	14900
4	1	11000
5	2	24600

Figure 2.4   The Stock Table

```
INSERT INTO CARS (MD_NUM, MD_NAME, STYLE, YEAR)
VALUES    (2, 'TOYOTA', 'SALOON', 1990);

INSERT INTO CARS (MD_NUM, MD_NAME, STYLE, YEAR)
VALUES    (3, 'BUICK', 'ESTATE', 1991);

INSERT INTO CARS (MD_NUM, MD_NAME, STYLE, YEAR)
VALUES    (4, 'NISSAN', 'VAN', 1992);

INSERT INTO CARS (MD_NUM, MD_NAME, STYLE, YEAR)

VALUES    (5, 'FORD', 'SALOON', 1993);
```

Four rows successfully inserted.

In the form of the INSERT statement that we have used above, you must specify three pieces of information. First, the name of the table to insert data into. Second, the names of the columns where data is to be added. Finally, you need to specify the actual data values.

We can add data to the SPECS table by:

INSERT INTO SPECS VALUES (1, 43, 'YES', '2L-4CYL');

INSERT INTO SPECS VALUES (2, 25, 'NO', '4L-V8');

INSERT INTO SPECS VALUES (3, 18, 'YES', '5L-V8');

INSERT INTO SPECS VALUES (4, 50, 'NO', '2L-4CYL');

INSERT INTO SPECS VALUES (5, 45, 'YES', '3L-V6');

Five rows successfully inserted.

and to the STOCK table by:

INSERT INTO STOCK VALUES   (1, 10, 4980);

INSERT INTO STOCK VALUES   (2, 3, 13865);

INSERT INTO STOCK VALUES   (3, 5, 14900);

INSERT INTO STOCK VALUES   (4, 1, 11000);

INSERT INTO STOCK VALUES   (5, 2, 24600);

Five rows successfully inserted.

The INSERT statements for the SPECS and the STOCK table did not use a value list. This is a shortcut which SQL allows you to use when you specify values for all the columns in each row.

2.6   Use the SELECT Statement: Extracting data from tables

The most important job of any database is to provide you with information. In SQL, the act of retrieving information is called querying the database. Information is retrieved from the database by using the SELECT statement.

In the previous two sections, we created the car dealership database, then added data to it. To retrieve the data from the CARS table of this database for example, you could use a SELECT statement. A SELECT statement is also called a query because it interrogates the database:

SELECT MD_NAME, STYLE, YEAR
FROM CARS;

MD_NAME	STYLE	YEAR
HONDA	COUPE	1983
TOYOTA	SALOON	1990
BUICK	ESTATE	1991
NISSAN	VAN	1992
FORD	SALOON	1993

The data retrieval requirements vary from user to user. For example, in our car dealership database, one user might want to know how many Nissan cars there are in stock while another might need to know how many cars there are which have a radio, eight cylinders and cost less than 10,000. As long as the information that you require is stored in the database in some form, you will be able to construct a form of SELECT statement which retrieves it. It is because of this flexibility that the SELECT statement is the most complex and also the most useful of all the SQL commands.

2.7   Use the UPDATE and DELETE Statements: Modifying data

In daily use, a database is a constantly changing store of data. The SQL commands which are used to modify data that is already in the database are the UPDATE and the DELETE commands. For example, to change the record of the Ford model in the CARS table to show the year of manufacture as 1989 and not 1993:

UPDATE CARS
  SET YEAR = 1989
  WHERE MD_NAME = 'FORD';

One row updated

We can express what this query is doing in words as 'Update the CARS table and set the YEAR column value to 1989 for all those records where the MD_NAME column value is FORD'. An important point to note is that UPDATE is capable of modifying the values of more than one record in a table. So if the CARS table had several Fords, then this statement would have changed the date of manufacture on all of them to 1989. You need to be wary of this when modifying values with UPDATE. The trick is to be so specific in the WHERE clause that only those records that you want to be changed are changed.

Another reason for wanting to modify the database is when deleting unwanted records from the tables SQL uses the DELETE command for this.

For example, if we decide that the Ford model in the CARS table is not available for sale, we can simply delete its record from the table by:

```
DELETE FROM CARS
  WHERE MD_NAME = 'FORD' AND YEAR = 1989;
```

One row deleted.

Just as with the UPDATE statement, care must be taken when using DELETE to ensure that only those records that you want deleted are actually deleted. The WHERE clause in this statement is a little more specific than the one we used in the last UPDATE statement. It asks SQL to delete only those records where the MD_NAME is Ford and also the YEAR is 1989. To confirm that the DELETE statement did remove the record for the Ford, we can query the CARS table:

```
SELECT *
  FROM CARS;
```

MD_NUM	MD_NAME	STYLE	YEAR
1	HONDA	COUPE	1983
2	TOYOTA	SALOON	1990
3	BUICK	ESTATE	1991
4	NISSAN	VAN	1992

The row for the Ford car has been deleted

2.8 Another Kind of Table, Called a Virtual Table: Views

The tables that you have been using up to now are called base tables. There is another kind of table, called a virtual table or view that is allowed for in

SQL. Base tables are database objects whose structure and the data they contain are both stored on disk. Views are tables whose contents are derived from base tables. Only their structure is stored on disk.

SQL's DML statements operate on views just as they do on base tables, but with one exception: when data is apparently added to, deleted or modified from a view, the actual data that is operated on is that in the underlying base tables that make up the view.

You can think of a view as a stencil or a window into a table or tables. Suppose that in a company personnel database, a staff table contains relevant work related information on employees such as department, supervisor, date joined, etc. The table might also contain sensitive information such as salary, home address and telephone number, etc. An excellent method of limiting casual user access to only the relevant work related information, and restrict access to the sensitive information would be to use a view.

In the used car dealership database for example, if the manager decides that he does not want everyone to see the price of the cars in the STOCK table, he could create a view called NO_PRICE:

```
CREATE VIEW NO_PRICE
  AS SELECT MD_NUM, QTY FROM STOCK;
```

View NO_PRICE successfully created.

Notice that the CREATE VIEW statement contains a SELECT statement as well. A view is in fact just a stored query that gets executed whenever the view is used as the subject of a command. The results of the query define the records 'held' in the view i.e. the data in the view.

Once created, the view's definition is stored by the DBMS and can be queried just like a regular base table. For example, to list all the 'rows' in NO_PRICE:

```
SELECT *
  FROM NO_PRICE;
```

MD_NUM	QTY
1	10
2	3
3	5
4	1
5	2

Notice that the view only displays two columns from the STOCK table. PRICE has been hidden from the user.

2.9 Prevent Access to Sensitive Information: Database security

As we have already seen, views can be used to prevent access to sensitive information in the database. Another method of enforcing security is by use of the GRANT and the REVOKE statements.

SQL operates on the concepts of user identification, ownership of database objects, and that of granting and revoking privileges from users. When a table is first created, it is owned by the user who created it. This means that the user who created the table is automatically given full privileges to operate on that table (INSERT data, UPDATE values, DELETE rows, etc). All other users are given no privileges on the table.

Let's see how this works. We will first create a view called NEW_CARS (which consists of cars whose year of manufacture is after 1990). We'll create this view under the user ID of JOE. Don't worry too much if the format of the CREATE VIEW appears a little strange. What it is doing is to temporarily set the user ID to JOE, then create the view, then revert back to the original user ID:

```
CREATE SCHEMA AUTHORIZATION JOE
  CREATE VIEW NEW_CARS
    AS SELECT * FROM CARS WHERE YEAR > 1990;
```

View NEW_CARS successfully created.

Now if we try to look at the data in the view:

```
SELECT *
  FROM NEW_CARS;
```

Error 98: User does not have the necessary SELECT privileges.

SQL tells us that we do not have the necessary privileges for this operation. We can confirm that the owner of the view, JOE, is allowed to look at the information by prefixing the JOE user-id to the viewname:

```
SELECT *
  FROM JOE.NEW_CARS;
```

MD_NUM	MD_NAME	STYLE	YEAR
3	BUICK	ESTATE	1991
4	NISSAN	VAN	1992

This query tells SQL that we know the user ID of the person who created the table is JOE, and we want it to use this for retrieving data from NEW_CARS.

3
Creating and Maintaining Tables

Before you can do anything in SQL, someone must first create a database structure composed of related tables, and then add data to those tables. The CREATE TABLE command is used to create new tables and is a part of SQL's DDL. This chapter starts by considering the DDL as defined by the ANSI/ISO standard. The later sections of this chapter describe how to create, alter and delete SQL tables. All the commands described in this section are concerned with operations on the tables themselves and do not directly affect the data stored in them.

Indexes are a method of speeding up the querying of tables, and these are also introduced in this chapter.

3.1 The ANSI Standard Makes Such a Distinction...: The DDL and the ANSI/ISO standard

The ANSI/ISO standard defines the SQL language as being composed of the Data Manipulation Language (DML) and the Data Definition Language (DDL). The DDL can be broadly considered as those SQL commands that operate on the structure of the database, i.e. the database objects such as tables, indexes and views. The DML on the other hand, can be thought of as those statements that operate on the data stored in the database tables themselves.

The ANSI/ISO standard makes such a distinction between these two aspects of SQL, that it considers them as two separate sub-languages. Indeed, once the database structure has been created, the ANSI/ISO standard does not even require the RDBMS to accept any DDL statements. This means that the ANSI/ISO standard separates the database development and creation activities from the database utilization activities. This is not the case in commercial SQL based RDBMSs where almost all allow the database development activities and the database utilization activities to be carried out jointly, with no separation between the DDL statements and the DML statements. This allows a minimal database to be created,

25

populated with data and used while at the same time, the structure of the database is broadened.

It is obvious that the ANSI/ISO method of separating the development activity from the utilization activity will lead to complications when it comes to altering the structure of the database, for instance, when it comes to removing a table. In fact, the ANSI/ISO standard does not even define the DROP TABLE statement to delete a table from the database or the ALTER TABLE statement to change the structure of a table. One of the few advantages of the ANSI/ISO method is that it forces you to adopt a rigorous systems analysis strategy before committing the final database design. Subsequent changes to the database structure will mean system downtime so you have to think hard to design the right system before you start using it.

3.2   Single and Multiple Database Architectures: The structure of SQL databases

The ANSI/ISO SQL standard specifies that the database schema consist of a single large database with tables which are owned by various users. The ownership of the tables sub-classifies them into different virtual database groups. This is shown in Figure 3.1. The tables owned by

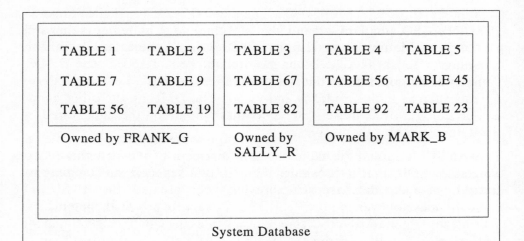

Figure 3.1   ANSI/ISO standard database structure

FRANK_G might be the Accounts (sub)database and those owned by MARK_B, the Suppliers (sub)database. Under the ANSI/ISO standard, both the Accounts tables and the Suppliers tables are part of the overall system database. All the tables in such single-database architectures can easily reference each other. The single-database architecture is used in both the Oracle and IBM's DB2 systems.

One of the disadvantages of the single-database architecture is that over time, as more and more tables are added to the system, the database becomes very big and bulky. Performing database administration tasks such as back-ups, performance analyzing. etc, on such large databases becomes a complex process, requiring the services of a dedicated database administrator. A database architecture which does not suffer from this disadvantage is the multiple-database architecture. Here, tables are organized into several distinct databases. This is shown in Figure 3.2. Although the data is split into several smaller, more manageable databases, the multiple-database architecture does suffer from a serious disadvantage. The tables in one database cannot (easily) contain foreign key references to keys in another database's table. The multiple-database architecture is used in Sybase, SQL Server and Ingres systems.

3.3   Creating a database table: The CREATE TABLE command

Creating database tables is done through the CREATE TABLE command. The CREATE TABLE command is one of three SQL statements that are part of the DDL and are used to manipulate the structure of tables that constitute a database. The other two are ALTER TABLE and DROP TABLE. We'll meet these later in this chapter.

The syntax of the CREATE TABLE statement is shown in Figure 3.3. The CREATE TABLE command creates an empty table-one with no records. The parameters that you must supply are name of the table, a list of the columns in the table and a description of the columns (data type, size, etc). A valid table must have at least one column but there is usually no upper limit specified.

ANSI/ISO SQL also allows you to create READ ONLY tables. This means that once created, SQL commands cannot be used to insert or update or delete any data in the tables. Creating READ ONLY tables only makes sense if some non-SQL process (an application program for example) is going to add the data.

The data types allowed in the column definitions vary considerably

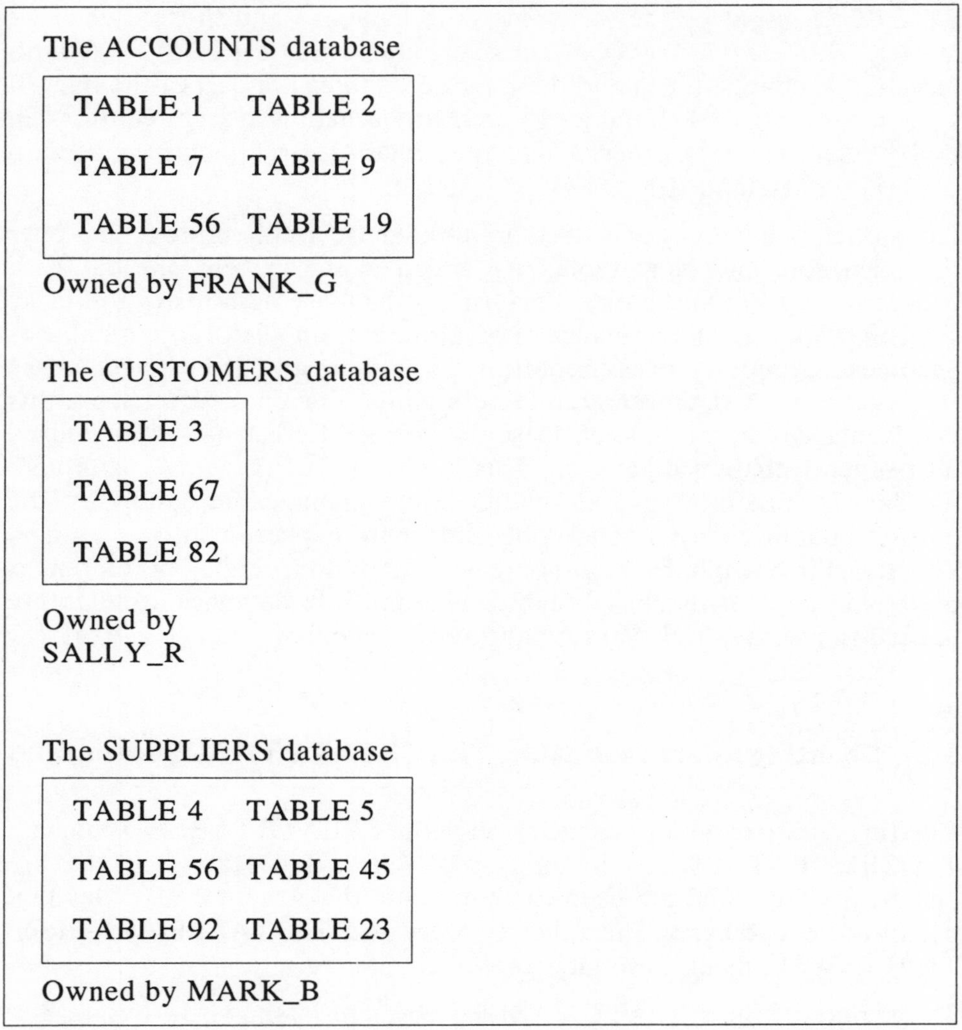

The ACCOUNTS database

TABLE 1	TABLE 2
TABLE 7	TABLE 9
TABLE 56	TABLE 19

Owned by FRANK_G

The CUSTOMERS database

TABLE 3
TABLE 67
TABLE 82

Owned by
SALLY_R

The SUPPLIERS database

TABLE 4	TABLE 5
TABLE 56	TABLE 45
TABLE 92	TABLE 23

Owned by MARK_B

Figure 3.2   Multiple-database structure

from product to product. Most commercial SQL systems support the ANSI data types as a minimum, and add additional types that are proprietary. The valid ANSI/ISO data types are given in Appendix A.

SQL Tips

> IBM's DB2 lets you store oriental language characters such as Kanji in fixed and variable length strings of 16-bit characters.

CREATE TABLE table [**READ_ONLY**]
(element { , element }) ;

table
The table name. This can be up to 24 characters.

element
column definition | unique constraint definition

column definition
col_name col_type [**NOT NULL**] [**UNIQUE INDEX**]

col_name
The name of the column can be up to 24 characters.

col_type
ANSI/ISO columns can be of the following type:
CHAR [(length)] |
VCHAR [(length)] |
NUMERIC [(precision [,scale])] |
DECIMAL [(precision [,scale])] |
INTEGER |
SMALLINT |
FLOAT [(precision)] |
DOUBLE PRECISION |
DATE

unique constraint definition
UNIQUE (col_name {, col_name }*)

Figure 3.3   Syntax of the CREATE TABLE command

The UNIQUE and the INDEX column modifiers both create indexes for the field to which they are applied. Indexes will be discussed in detail in the next section. The NOT NULL column modifier adds the condition that a record cannot be inserted into the table if no value is supplied for this particular field.

In SQL, tables are owned by the user who created them. Initially, only the table's owner is allowed to perform any operations involving that table. Other users must refer to the table by preceding the table name with the owner/user's ID. A table which is meant for use by all users can be created under a special user identifier known as PUBLIC. Tables created under PUBLIC allow all users on the system to access them. We came across the concept of ownership and privileges briefly in Chapter 2. The subject of table ownership is discussed more fully in the chapter on database security.

The names of tables which are owned by any given user must all be different. Some systems extend this so that the names of all the tables in the whole system must be different from each other. This also applies to column names within a table, but separate tables can however, have repeating column names.

We will be using a database based on a university administration system throughout this book. The database consists of five tables: STUDENTS, LECTURERS, SUBJECTS, EXAMS and DEPARTMENTS. The whole database will be created and used in stages as we progress through the chapters. The structure of the tables as well as the data in them is shown in Figure 3.4. Appendix B gives an in depth description of this sample database.

Let's begin by creating the first table in our university admin. system, the STUDENTS table:

```
CREATE SCHEMA AUTHORIZATION PUBLIC
CREATE TABLE STUDENTS    (
          SURNAME        CHAR (15) NOT NULL,
          FIRST_NAME     CHAR (15),
          D_O_B          DATE,
          STUDENT_NO     INTEGER NOT NULL UNIQUE,
          DEPT_NO        INTEGER,
          YEAR           DECIMAL (2)  );
```

Table STUDENTS successfully created.

This query instructs the system to create a new table called STUDENTS with six fields. When the table is first created, it contains no data rows. We have used CREATE TABLE in conjunction with the CREATE SCHEMA statement because the ANSI/ISO standard specifies that the CREATE SCHEMA statement forms the basis of the CREATE TABLE statement as well as the CREATE VIEW and the GRANT statements. The CREATE SCHEMA statement tells SQL who the owner of the newly created table is to be and this can be different from the current user-id.

SURNAME	FIRST_NAME	D_O_B	STUDENT_NO	DEPT_NO	YEAR
Duke	Fitzroy	11-26-1970	1	4	2
Al-Essawy	Zaid M A	11-26-1970	2	4	2
Ayton	Phil J M A	07-13-1967	3	3	1
Patel	Mahesh	12-07-1970	4	2	1
Jones	Gareth P Y	01-24-1970	5	2	1
Scott	Gavin T J	02-20-1971	6	2	2
Baker	Abu-Mia	03-13-1971	7	4	1
Brown	Joseph P A	04-19-1970	8	3	3
Monkhouse	Robert Jones	05-23-1967	9	1	1
Grimm	Hans Johan	06-21-1971	10	2	1
Gyver	Sue L J V	07-30-1968	11	4	2
Hung-Sun	Jimmy Lau	08-11-1969	12	1	3
Middleton	Jane P	09-14-1971	13	1	3
Mulla	Farook F U	10-24-1968	14	3	2
Layton	Hugh	11-16-1971	15	5	1
Wickes	Wendy Y Y W	12-05-1969	16	1	1

THE STUDENTS TABLE

SURNAME	INITL	LECT_NO	DEPT_NO	SUB_N	GRADE	PAY	JOINED
Jones	R A	1	1	2	E	24000	03-25-1990
Scrivens	T R	2	3	1	D	31800	09-30-1986
Nizamuddin	W M	3	3	4	A	86790	05-26-1969
Campbell	J G	4	5	3	C	43570	02-23-1980
Ramanujan	S	5	4	5	C	40900	01-01-1985
Finley	G Y	6	4	5	D	34210	03-28-1960

THE LECTURERS TABLE

SUB_NO	SUB_NAME	DEPT_NO	CREDITS	PASS
1	Mathematics	1	2	65
2	English Lit	2	1	60
3	Engineering Drwg	1	1	71
4	Basic Accounts	3	1	67
5	Industrial Law	4	2	52
6	Organic Chemistry	5	3	57
7	Physiology	6	3	78
8	Anatomy	6	1	74
9	Electronics	1	3	71
10	Marketing	3	2	56

THE SUBJECTS TABLE

Figure 3.4   The University Administration Database

SUB_NO	STUDENT_NO	MARK	DATE_TAKEN
1	1	76	05-23-1984
9	1	42	05-20-1984
3	1	67	05-15-1984
2	2	52	06-05-1984
2	3	89	06-08-1984
2	3	51	05-11-1984
4	4	34	05-11-1984
10	4	49	06-26-1984
5	5	62	05-03-1984
5	6	70	05-17-1984
5	7	36	05-23-1984
5	8	52	05-20-1984
6	9	67	05-15-1984
6	10	82	06-05-1984
6	11	73	06-08-1984
7	12	27	05-11-1984
8	12	56	05-11-1984
8	13	67	06-26-1984
7	13	63	05-03-1984

THE EXAMS TABLE

DEPT_NO	DEPT_NAME	HEAD	BUDGET	P_BUDGET
1	Engineering	59	5780000	6200000
2	Arts & Humanities	23	753000	643000
3	Management Studies	3	2510000	1220000
4	Industrial Law	12	78000	210000
5	Physical Sciences	18	4680000	4250000
6	Medicine	67	6895000	6932000

THE DEPARTMENTS TABLE

Figure 3.4   University Administration Database – Continued

Strictly speaking, ANSI SQL does not allow the CREATE TABLE statement to be used without the CREATE SCHEMA clause but almost all popular versions of SQL allow CREATE TABLE statements to be used without the preceding CREATE SCHEMA clause. In this case, the current authorization identifier will be assigned as the owner of the table.

The order in which the columns are defined is important. The column order is the default order in which the results are displayed whenever the table is queried.

In the STUDENTS table, SURNAME, FIRST_NAME, D_O_B, . . . are all column names. Columns in the same table must each have unique column names but columns in different tables can have the same name.

The CREATE TABLE statement must define the data type for each column, immediately after the column name. Data types define the type of the data that can be stored in the column. For example, if a column is defined as being DECIMAL data type, than it will only hold decimal values. Trying to store text strings in the column will cause an error. Appendix A describes the ANSI/ISO standard data types, but these are not the only types that are available in commercial SQL systems. Almost all the popular SQL RDBMSs support the ANSI/ISO data types as a minimum set but add to it substantially. Some of the more common additional data types include money, date and boolean (to store true/false values).

SQL Tips

DB2 suports three different date and time data types: DATE, TIME and TIMESTAMP which is used to specify an instant in time.

Now let's construct the other tables that form the sample database. The LECTURERS table holds details of the teaching staff at the university. To create the LECTURERS table:

```
CREATE TABLE LECTURERS  (
        SURNAME         CHAR (15)       NOT NULL,
        INITL           CHAR (4),
        LECT_NO         INTEGER NOT NULL,
        DEPT_NO         INTEGER,
        SUB_NO          INTEGER,
        GRADE           CHAR (1),
        PAY             DECIMAL (6),
        JOINED          DATE,
        UNIQUE (SURNAME,        LECT_NO) );
```

Table LECTURERS successfully created.

Notice that this time, the unique constraint definition is at the end of the CREATE TABLE statement. ANSI/ISO SQL allows you to specify a group of columns as being UNIQUE in this way. This differs from using the UNIQUE keyword as a column modifier in that SQL considers the combination of fields (SURNAME and LECT_NO in this case) to be unique.

SQL Tips

> OS/2 Extended Edition does not support date arithmetic.

The SUBJECTS table holds the details of the subjects taught at the university. To create the SUBJECTS table:

```
CREATE TABLE SUBJECTS    (
   SUB_NO                  INTEGER NOT FULL UNIQUE,
   SUB_NAME                CHAR (20),
   DEPT_NO                 INTEGER,
   CREDITS                 NUMERIC (2),
   PASS                    NUMERIC (2) );
```

Table SUBJECTS successfully created.

The EXAMS table holds the details of the exams taken by the students and the results they achieved. To create the exams table:

```
CREATE TABLE EXAMS       (
   SUB_NO                  INTEGER NOT NULL,
   STUDENT_NO              INTEGER NOT NULL,
   MARK                    DECIMAL (3),
   DATE_TAKEN              DATE );
```

Table EXAMS successfully created.

The DEPARTMENTS table holds the details of all the university departments. To create the departments table:

```
CREATE TABLE DEPARTMENTS    (
   DEPT_NO                 INTEGER NOT NULL,
   DEPT_NAME               CHAR (20),
   HEAD                    INTEGER,
   BUDGET                  DECIMAL (10),
```

```
P_BUDGET                    DECIMAL (10)
UNIQUE (DEPT_NO) );
```

Table DEPARTMENTS successfully.

SQL Tips

Oracle's DATE type stores both date and time down to a second accuracy. In this respect, it is similar to DB2's TIMESTAMP type.

3.4 Apply Restrictions to Groups of Columns: Column and table modifiers

The CREATE TABLE command allows you to specify column modifiers, such as NOT NULL for the DEPT_NO column in DEPARTMENTS and UNIQUE for the STUDENT_NO column in STUDENTS. These modifiers tell SQL to control the data that can be input into the column. The CREATE TABLE command also lets you specify table modifiers which apply restrictions to groups of columns such as the UNIQUE table modifier in the LECTURERS table definition which applies the UNIQUE constraint to both the SURNAME and the LECT_NO fields jointly.

3.4.1 The NOT NULL modifier

The NOT NULL modifier prevents NULL (a token that designates a column as being empty) values from appearing in the column. This means that a row cannot be added to the table if values for the NOT NULL columns is not supplied. NOT NULL is usually used for primary keys, for which there must be a value for all rows in the table.

3.4.2 The UNIQUE modifier

The UNIQUE modifier is used in the STUDENTS table on the SURNAME and the STUDENT_NO fields. UNIQUE ensures that the values entered into the column are all different from each other. Rows cannot be added to the table if the value for a UNIQUE column is already in the table. It only makes sense to apply UNIQUE to columns that are also declared NOT NULL. If this is not done, then only one row will be allowed to have a NULL value for that column because the UNIQUE constraint will prevent other NULLs from being entered. Subsequent rows will thus have the NOT NULL constraint applied by default.

SQL Tips

> Most commercial SQL systems use the non-standard CREATE INDEX statement to specify a column as being unique.

3.4.3 The INDEX modifier

The INDEX modifier is not part of the ANSI/ISO standard but is quite common in commercial SQL systems. INDEX causes an index to be created based on the values in the column, which greatly speeds up query processing. Almost all commercial SQL systems also create an index for columns that are defined as UNIQUE. Index maintenance is taken care of by the DBMS, and so the user is not always aware of when indexes are being created.

3.4.4 The PRIMARY KEY modifier

The PRIMARY KEY modifier is a relatively new feature in SQL which is not available in all systems. The modifier enables us to tell SQL which columns in our tables are the primary keys. Up to now, we have been dealing with primary keys as logical concepts only. This modifier enables us to extend this so that we can formally define primary keys. For example, in the SUBJECTS table, we said that the SUB_NO column is the primary key. To formally define this, the CREATE TABLE statement would be:

```
CREATE TABLE SUBJECTS    (
   SUB_NO              INTEGER NOT NULL,
   SUB_NAME            CHAR (20),
   DEPT_NO             INTEGER,
   CREDITS             NUMERIC (2),
   PASS                NUMERIC (2),
   PRIMARY KEY (SUB_NO) );
```

Table SUBJECTS successfully created.

Note that a column must be declared as NOT NULL before the PRIMARY KEY modifier can be applied to it.

3.4.5 The FOREIGN KEY modifier

This modifier is closely related to the PRIMARY KEY modifier. Most tables contain references to primary keys in other tables, called foreign keys. SQL allows you to define these relations when you create the table. In the SUBJECTS table for example, the DEPT_NO column is a foreign key. Thus a more complete CREATE TABLE statement would be:

```
CREATE TABLE SUBJECTS      (
   SUB_NO                   INTEGER NOT NULL,
   SUB_NAME                 CHAR (20),
   DEPT_NO                  INTEGER,
   CREDITS                  NUMERIC (2),
   PASS                     NUMERIC (2),
   PRIMARY KEY (SUB_NO),
   FOREIGN KEY (DEPT_NO)
   REFERENCE DEPARTMENTS );
```

Table SUBJECTS successfully created.

This statement tells SQL that the DEPT_NO column is a foreign key in this table what references the DEPARTMENTS table. Since there can only be one primary key for each table, the DBMS knows that the DEPT_NO column (foreign key in SUBJECTS) references the DEPT_NO column (primary key) in the DEPARTMENTS table.

3.4.6 The DEFAULT modifier

The ANSI/ISO standard allows you to define default values that columns should have. Usually, if no value is supplied for a column, then it is assigned the NULL value. The DEFAULT column modifier overrides this. In the SUBJECTS table for example, if the default pass mark for an exam is 65%, then we can set this at the CREATE TABLE stage by:

```
CREATE TABLE SUBJECTS      (
   SUB_NO                   INTEGER NOT NULL,
   SUB_NAME                 CHAR (20),
   DEPT_NO                  INTEGER,
   CRDITS                   NUMERIC (2),
   PASS                     NUMERIC (2) DEFAULT 65,
   PRIMARY KEY (SUB_NO),
   FOREIGN KEY (DEPT_NO)
   REFERENCE DEPARTMENTS );
```

Table SUBJECTS successfully created.

You should use default values where you would otherwise have to type repetitive data. Such as the city column in an address table, where most of the values might be for the same city. Default values can also be used as an alternative to NULLs. NULL values appear false in any comparison operations and hence tend to be excluded in a lot of SQL queries where their inclusion might give more meaningful results. Use DEFAULT to ensure that all values in the column are non-null.

3.4.7 The CHECK modifier

Some of the columns in the tables you create will have a range of acceptable values or the values may need to be entered in a particular format. The CHECK modifier allows you to tell SQL about these acceptable values or format. In the EXAMS table for example, the CREDITS awarded for a subject must be greater than 0 and the maximum number of credits that can be awarded for any subject is 10. This can be expressed in the CREATE TABLE statement as:

```
CREATE TABLE SUBJECTS      (
   SUB_NO                    INTEGER NOT NULL,
   SUB_NAME                  CHAR (20),
   DEPT_NO                   INTEGER,
   CREDITS                   NUMERIC (2) CHECK
            (CREDITS > 0 AND CREDITS <= 10),
   PASS                      NUMERIC (2) DEFAULT 65,
   PRIMARY KEY (SUB_NO),
   FOREIGN KEY (SUB_NO)
   REFERENCE DEPARTMENTS );
```

As with the other column modifiers, CHECK can also be applied as a table constraint. This is useful where CHECK is to be applied to more than one column. Thus for the LECTURERS table, if a salary of 100,000 or more is only allowed if the lecturer is on seniority grade A or B, then we could use CHECK as a table modifier:

```
CREATE TABLE LECTURERS   (
   SURNAME                  CHAR (15) NOT NULL,
   INITL                    CHAR (4),
   LECT_NO                  INTEGER NOT NULL,
   DEPT_NO                  INTEGER,
   SUB_NO                   INTEGER,
   GRADE                    CHAR (1),
```

```
PAY                         DECIMAL (6),
JOINED                      DATE
UNIQUE    (SURNAME, LECT_NO),
CHECK     (PAY < 100000 OR GRADE <= 'B') ) ;
```

Table LECTURERS successfully created.

3.5 Indexes are Ordered for Extremely Fast Searches: Indexes

An index is a database object created and maintained by the DBMS. It is essentially a list of the contents of a column or group of columns. Indexes are ordered so that extremely fast searches can be conducted through them to find data. The rows in tables are not ordered in any particular sequence, they are merely stored in the order in which they were inserted into the table. As most large SQL databases have tables with thousands or even millions of rows, searching through them to find particular values can become quite time consuming. Indexes speed up this search process by keeping a sorted list of values which the DBMS can search through.

How does the DBMS use indexes? To answer this question, let's consider an example. Figure 3.5 shows a table in a corporate database. Assume that it holds records of all potential suppliers listed for all the cities of the world. If we run the query for an unindexed table, SQL would need to look through 99003 rows before it found the record for Hyderabad, which we wanted. In executing such a query, SQL starts at record 1 and checks if the condition CITY = 'HYBD' is true. If it is, then the record is retrieved into the results table. SQL then moves on to record 2 and repeats the process. This is done until it reaches the last row in the table.

Now let's see how the query is speeded up by using an index. If the CITY field was indexed, then the index will keep an ordered list of all the data in the CITY column as well as information that tells the DBMS where to find each record on disk. Figure 3.6 shows how the index is organized. To resolve the query with condition CITY = 'HYBD', the DBMS only needs to scan through the index and find the first entry for HYBD. The index tells the DBMS where to look in the table to find the actual record. The index holds all the entries for HYBD sequentially, and so the database can quickly refer to the index to find all the rows where CITY = 'HYBD'.

Although indexing tables has many advantages, it also has disadvantages.

```
QUERY:    SELECT * FROM SUPPLIERS
                WHERE CITY = 'HYBD';


. . . C_NUM  QTY   CITY . . . . . .
       ─────  ───   ────
       99001  934   N.Y.
       99002  467   LOND
       99003   12   HYBD  <- - - - - The query needs to look through
       99004  456   L.A.     |     99005 rows to find these record.
       99005   23   HYBD  <- - -

The SUPPLIERS table
```

Figure 3.5   Searching through an unindexed table

Indexes use up additional disk space, and also when tables are added to, deleted from or the values of indexed columns are modified, the DBMS needs to maintain the index as well. This addition makes INSERT, UPDATE and DELETE commands run slower.

Indexes are created with the non ANSI/ISO CREATE INDEX command. On most systems, this command also lets you specify the name of the index to be created. Although you will not be allowed to directly manipulate the index in any way, the index name is useful when you want to delete the index.

To create an index on the CITY column of the SUPPLIERS table in Figure 3.6 for example:

CREATE INDEX SUPP_CTY_IDX
  ON SUPPLIERS (CITY) ;

Index SUPP_CTY_IDX successfully created.

We could have also used CREATE UNIQUE INDEX instead of CREATE INDEX. The UNIQUE keyword tells SQL that the CITY columns can only contain unique values. Recall that the ANSI/ISO standard allows you to specify UNIQUE as a column modifier in the CREATE TABLE statement itself.

As CREATE INDEX is not a part of the ANSI/ISO standard, systems vendors allow many additional clauses to this command that deal with the physical characteristics of the index to be created.

```
KEY-FIELD LOCATION
.
.
.
HAMBURG    0033433344
HELSINKI   0042124442
HYBD       0001276900
HYBD       0001276902
JHBG       0034412344
KBUL       0056789877
.
.
.
```

The KEY-FIELD is an ordered list of the CITIES column in the SUPPLIERS table.

The LOCATION is a number that tells the DBMS exactly where on the disk to find each record.

Figure 3.6   The organization of data in an index

Indexes created with the CREATE INDEX command can later be deleted by the DROP INDEX command. For example, to get rid of the SUPP_CTY_IDX index:

DROP INDEX SUPP_CTY_IDX ;

Index SUPP_CTY_IDX successfully dropped.

3.6   Changing the Structure of a Table: The ALTER TABLE Command.

The ALTER TABLE command allows a user to change the structure of a table. New columns can be added with the ADD clause. Existing columns can be modified with the MODIFY clause. Columns can be removed from a table by using the DROP clause. The syntax of the ALTER TABLE command is shown in Figure 3.7.

```
ALTER TABLE tbl_name
ADD (
column definition [ BEFORE col name ]
{ , column definition [BEFORE col name ] }* )

DROP ( col name { , col name }* )

MODIFY ( column definition { , column definition }* ) ;
```

tbl_name
The name of the table to alter.

col_name
The name of the column to alter.

column definition
See the CREATE TABLE section for the syntax of column definition.

Figure 3.7   The syntax of the ALTER TABLE statement

The ALTER TABLE command is not part of the ANSI/ISO standard. According to ANSI/ISO reasoning, you should have designed your tables on paper first, and subsequent alterations to them should not be necessary. The non-standard nature of the ALTER TABLE command means that, all the commercial dialects of SQL implement different clauses and command syntax.

On most systems, you are allowed to add more than one column with a single ALTER TABLE command. However, you should not count on this feature. To add the departmental phone number column to the DEPARTMENTS table for example:

```
ALTER TABLE DEPARTMENTS
ADD (PHONE_NO CHAR (12) BEFORE HEAD) ;
```

Table DEPARTMENTS successfully altered.

This query alters the structure of the DEPARTMENTS table by adding an additional column called PHONE_NO The BEFORE clause is optional and tells SQL to position the new column immediately before the column

DEPT_NO	DEPT_NAME	PHONE_NO	HEAD	BUDGET	P_BUDGET
1	Engineering	?	59	5790000	6200000
2	Art & Humanities	?	23	753000	643000
3	Management Studies	?	34	2510000	1220000
4	Industrial Law	?	12	78000	210000
5	Physical Sciences	?	18	4680000	4250000
6	Medicine	?	67	6895000	69320D0

The ? in the PHONE NO column indicates a NULL value added to the column values for all extant rows.

Figure 3.8 The structure of the modified DEPARTMENTS table

called HEAD. The new structure of the table is shown in Figure 3.8. If the BEFORE clause is omitted, then the new column will be added at the end of the existing columns i.e. after P_BUDGET Most dialects of SQL set the values in the newly added column to NULL for all extant rows, but as ever, this should not always be assumed for all systems.

Most forms of ALTER TABLE also allow you to delete columns from tables. Thus:

ALTER TABLE DEPARTMENTS DROP (PHONE_NO);

Table DEPARTMENTS successfully altered.

will remove the PHONE_NO column from the DEPARTMENTS table.

Once the column is dropped, then the data is lost, it cannot be retrieved.

The MODIFY clause of the ALTER TABLE command allows you to modify the UNIQUE or the NOT NULL status of a column. To make more extensive changes to a column, you should DROP it and then ADD it with the changes incorporated.

You should only modify the UNIQUE or NOT NULL status of a column if the table is empty. If the UNIQUE or the NOT NULL status of a column is modified on a non-empty table, an error may occur because duplicate or NULL values of that column may already exist in the table data. Changing the structure of a table already populated with data is risky to say the least. On corporate databases especially, even on the best administered system, there are always some views created by users or embedded SQL programs which may no longer function because they relied on the previous structure of the modified table. Modifications need to be carefully planned and implemented.

For a well designed table, you should never need to change the constraints (UNIQUE, NOT NULL, etc.) on a table column and you should only use the ALTER TABLE command as a last resort, when all else fails. An alternative to using the ALTER TABLE command is to simply create a new table with the modified structure and populate it with data from the old table. (A simple way of doing this is to use the INSERT command with a SELECT * query. This is discussed in full in the next chapter).

Remember that in order to be able to use the ALTER TABLE command, in the first place, you must be either the table's owner or have been granted ALL PRIVILEGES for the table by the owner.

3.7   Remove Redundant Tables from the Database: The DROP TABLE Command

As your database evolves, you will eventually want to remove redundant tables from the database. The DROP TABLE command is used to delete tables. Some DBMSs require that the table to be eliminated must be empty before it can be dropped from the database. This is used as a safety feature, to prevent accidental deletion of tables that are still in use. You should not count on this and should always delete tables with extreme care.

Since the DROP TABLE option removes all trace of the table as far as SQL is concerned, it is important to ensure that no command files, embedded SQL programs or columns from other tables refer to the dropped table's fields in the form of foreign keys. If the deleted table is accessed by views, then you will obviously need to ensure that the views are removed before the table. Most commercial implementations of SQL are smart enough to prevent you from deleting tables that have associated views.

To delete the STUDENTS table for example:

DROP TABLE STUDENTS ;

Table STUDENTS successfully dropped.

Although DROP TABLE is not part of the ANSI standard (ANSI specifies no means of destroying table definitions) it is nonetheless, a very useful command for restructuring and maintaining your database.

4

Querying SQL Tables

A query is a method of interrogating an SQL database. It is used to tell the DBMS what information you want it to retrieve from the database and also how you want the data to appear. When you think about it, the only reason for storing and maintaining a database of information is to make it easy to get at the information that you need, when you need it. One of the most important functions of any query language is to make the retrieval of information as easy and also as powerful as possible for the user. Data retrieval needs to be easy because most of the time, the people who query the database are not the same people who programmed the database. Users are not interested in the technicalities of how the database is organized or how it is managed. The query language needs to have easy to understand (preferably plain English) commands that users can use intuitively. The query language also needs to be powerful because it needs to be capable of providing users with all the information that they may want. As the DBMS has no idea of what the user queries are going to be beforehand, the language constructs must be powerful enough to deal with all the requests the users are likely to make.

4.1 The most basic query: The Simple SELECT statement

The SELECT statement allows you to specify the data that you want to retrieve, what order to arrange the data, what calculations to perform on the retrieved data and many, many more operations. As it's the only SQL verb that enables you to query the database and SQL is a query language, it is necessarily the most complex of all SQL commands. ANSI/ISO SQL allows up to six different clauses in the SELECT statement of which the first two are mandatory. The syntax of the full SELECT statement is shown in Figure 4.1.

The simple SELECT statement, as the name implies, is the most elementary form of query which uses only the mandatory clauses of the full SELECT. It only requires you to supply two pieces of information. First, the

SELECT [**DISTINCT**] field_expression { , field expression }*
FROM table_spec { , table_spec }*
[**WHERE** search_condition]
[**ORDER BY** field_name {, field_name }*]
[**GROUP BY** field_name {, field_name }*]
[**HAVING condition**]
;

field_expression
The field_expression may be one of the following:
- Field name e.g. SNO, S.SNO.
- ANSI aggregate function SUM( ), AVG( ), MIN( ), MAX( ) and
COUNT( ).
- * is a special field_expression which means select all fields.

table_spec
The name for the table(s) to select from.

search_condition
The WHERE search condition specifies what records are to be
retrieved in the SELECT.

field_name
Field names should have meaningful names that describe the contents
of the field.

condition
The HAVING condition is used to eliminate some groups from a
SELECT query.

Figure 4.1 The syntax of the SELECT statement

columns that you wish to see, and second, the name of the table that the
columns are in. For example, this query retrieves all the rows in the
DEPARTMENTS table:

SELECT DEPT_NO, DEPT_NAME, HEAD, BUDGET, P_BUDGET
FROM DEPARTMENTS ;

DEPT_NO	DEPT_NAME	HEAD	BUDGET	P_BUDGET
1	Engineering	59	5780000	6200000
2	Arts & Humanities	23	753000	643000
3	Management Studies	3	2510000	1220000
4	Industrial Law	12	78000	210000
5	Physical Sciences	18	4680000	4250000
6	Medicine	67	6895000	6932000

You can specify more than one table name in the FROM clause, but in this case, SQL will produce a listing of all the rows from the second named table for each row in the first named table. This is known as the cartesian product of the tables. For example:

SELECT DEPT_NAME, SUB_NAME
FROM DEPARTMENTS, SUBJECTS ;

DEPT_NAME	SUB_NAME
Engineering	Mathematics
Enngineering	English Lit
Engineering	Engineering Drawing
Engineering	Basic Accounts
Engineering	Industrial Law
Engineering	Organic Chemistry
Engineering	Physiology
Engineering	Anatomy
Engineering	Electronics
Engineering	Marketing
Arts & Humanities	Mathematics
Arts & Humanities	English Lit
Arts & Humanities	Engineering Drawing
Arts & Humanities	Basic Accounts
Arts & Humanities	Industrial Law
Arts & Humanities	Organic Chemistry
Arts & Humanities	Physiology
Arts & Humanities	Anatomy

The information retrieved by a cartesian product query can quickly grow if more than two tables are specified. For three tables of 100 rows each, a cartesian product SELECT will produce 1 million result rows. In most cases, the results are not of much use as they do not easily relate to real life situations.

To find out what the simple SELECT does, let's have a closer look at what the query we've just used is telling the DBMS; 'SELECT the DEPT_NO, the DEPT_NAME, the HEAD, the BUDGET and the P_BUDGET columns FROM the DEPARTMENTS table'. When you read it out like this, it is obvious what information this query is requesting from the DBMS. In most versions of interpreted SQL, the results are displayed as soon as the DBMS finishes executing the query. In most cases, the results appear on the screen as they are shown in this book. Column names are at the top with the columns shown in the order in which they were specified in the SELECT statement. If more columns are specified in the SELECT statement than can fit on the screen, on some systems they are split up on two or more lines. Other systems allow you to scroll up, down, left or right through the results by using the arrow keys. The second method is better because when results columns are split up on different lines, the formatting is lost and data appears to be displayed haphazardly.

The query result rows are not listed in any particular order. The DBMS just lists the rows in the order in which it comes across them in the table.

Note that all SQL queries (and other statements too, for that matter) end with the semicolon character. Newline can be used to format the query into clauses so that it is easier to understand what the query is doing when you refer to it several weeks later say. Most SQL interpreters and programs treat the newline and the tab characters as equivalent to the space character. You can type all SQL statements on a long single line if you wanted. To tell SQL that you have finished entering the query, you must type the semicolon character at the end.

To retrieve all the columns from a table, SQL allows you to use the asterisk, *, character as a shortcut. Thus the following query is exactly the same as the previous query where we retrieved all the columns from the DEPARTMENTS table:

```
SELECT *
FROM DEPARTMENTS ;
```

DEPT_NO	DEPT_NAME	HEAD	BUDGET	P_BUDGET
1	Engineering	59	5780000	6200000
2	Arts & Humanities	23	753000	643000
3	Management Studies	3	2510000	1220000
4	Industrial Law	12	78000	210000
5	Physical Sciences	18	4680000	4250000
6	Medicine	67	6895000	6932000

In place of the asterisk, you should read 'all the fields' in the SELECT statement. Notice how the columns in the results appear in the order in which they were defined when the table was created.

So far, we have looked at SELECT statements that retrieve all the columns from a table. In most cases, we are only interested in certain columns in a table. SQL allows us to specify these columns in the first clause of the SELECT. As an example, say we wanted to look at the pass mark for each subject in the SUBJECTS table, we are only interested in the SUB_NAME and the PASS columns in the SUBJECTS table:

```
SELECT PASS, SUB_NAME
FROM SUBJECTS ;
```

PASS	SUB_NAME
65	Mathematics
60	English Lit
71	Engineering Drawing
67	Basic Accounts
52	Industrial Law
57	Organic Chemistry
78	Physiology
74	Anatomy
71	Electronics
56	Marketing

If a column list is used the columns in the results table appear in the order in which they are specified in the SELECT. You can use this fact to change the order in which the columns appear in the results.

Leaving columns out of the SELECT statement only affects the results of the query. It does not affect the data in the named table in any way.

As well as simple column names, the SELECT clause also lets you use scalar expressions and string constants. Scalar expressions are simple calculations performed on numeric type column values. The results of the calculation are displayed in the results table as columns. For example, we can use a scalar expression using the annual pay field to display the monthly pay for each lecturer:

```
SELECT SURNAME, PAY, (PAY / 12)
FROM LECTURERS ;
```

SURNAME	PAY	
Jones	24000	2000
Scrivens	31800	2650
Nizamuddin	86790	7232
Campbell	43570	3630
Ramanujan	40900	3408
Finley	34210	2850

The third column in the results table has been generated as a direct result of the PAY / 12 calculation that we specified. The data in this column is not actually stored in any table, but has been calculated by SQL. In most versions of SQL, expressions are only allowed to use the addition, subtraction, multiplication and division functions. The fields used in expressions must be numeric type. Notice that the heading of the generated column is the expression that we used in the SELECT clause. This feature depends on the particular version of SQL that you use. Some dialects of SQL have blank headings for calculated columns.

SQL lets you use string constants in the column list to output text messages. When you use string constants, the string value will appear in the column position for each row of the results table. As with all string values, constants must be inside single quotes:

```
SELECT SUB_NAME'has pass mark of', PASS, '%'
FROM SUBJECTS ;
```

SUB_NAME		PASS	
Mathematics	has pass mark of	65	%
English Lit	has pass mark of	60	%
Engineering Drwg	has pass mark of	71	%
Basic Accounts	has pass mark of	67	%
Industrial Law	has pass mark of	52	%
Organic Chemistry	has pass mark of	57	%
Physiology	has pass mark of	78	%
Anatomy	has pass mark of	74	%
Electronics	has pass mark of	71	%
Marketing	has pass mark of	56	%

SQL Tips

SQL Server, Informix and dBase IV accept string constants enclosed in double quotes (". . .").

In this query, the use of string constants is not very elegant. The same comment appears for all the result rows. Constants are most useful when used with aggregate functions that produce a single calculated value based on the data in tables for example:

SELECT 'The average pass mark is', AVG(PASS), '% per subject'
FROM SUBJECTS ;

	AVG(PASS)	
The average pass mark is	65.1	% per subject

AVG(PASS) is an aggregate function which calculates the average value of the PASS column. This will be discussed further in a later section.

ANSI/ISO SQL defines SELECT statements as part of the DML. ANSI/ISO SQL further defines DML commands as having the ability to change the data in the database. SELECT by itself, cannot alter data in the database and so it is not strictly a part of the DML. Database data is modified only when SELECT is used in conjunction with other DML commands such as INSERT and UPDATE. It is best to think of the SELECT as being in a category by itself.

SELECT lets you use the DISTINCT keyword to eliminate duplicate rows from the query results. Consider the DEPT_NO column in the STUDENTS table. This gives the department number that each student belongs to. If we simply wanted to know which departments are represented in the STUDENTS table, we could use the DISTINCT argument to remove repeat values for this column from the results table:

SELECT DISTINCT DEPT_NO
FROM STUDENTS ;

DEPT_NO
```
       1
       2
       3
       4
       5
```

DISTINCT is very useful in queries where you simply want to know if a value is present in a table and are not interested in how many times it occurs. DISTINCT itself can only be used once in a SELECT statement. However, you can specify more than one column after DISTINCT. In this case, SQL will eliminate those rows where the values are the same in all the columns.

The opposite of DISTINCT is ALL. This is the default that SQL assumes if neither is specified. In practice, ALL is not used. It is understood that if DISTINCT is absent, then the default, ALL is in effect and all columns, including duplicates will be displayed in the results table.

4.1.1 Calculated columns

As well as using simple column names, you can also specify scalar mathematical expressions. These are known as calculated columns; for example:

SELECT DEPT_NAME, (BUDGET + 15000), (BUDGET - P_BUDGET),
       (BUDGET * 2.25), (BUDGET / 4.5) FROM DEPARTMENTS

DEPT_NAME

Engineering	5795000	−420000	65025000	1284444.4
Arts & Humanities	768000	110000	8471250	167333.3
Management Studies	2525000	1290000	28237500	557777.7
Industrial Law	93000	−132000	877500	17333.3
Physical Sciences	4695000	430000	52650000	1040000
Medicine	6910000	-37000	77568750	1532222.2

This query demonstrates the use of calculated columns. You are allowed to use the addition, subtraction, multiplication and division mathematical functions with both numeric constants and column names as long as the columns involved are numeric type columns. Trying to use non-numeric column types will cause an error.

4.2 Selecting rows for output: The WHERE clause

One of the most useful feature of the SQL query is that it allows you to selectively retrieve only those rows that interest you. In a large database, with thousands of rows in each table, you may only be interested in a handful of records at any time. The WHERE clause of the SELECT statement lets you specify a predicate, which tells SQL what records are to appear in the results. A predicate is a logical expression that can be either true or false. As an example, consider in the DEPARTMENTS table, the predicate 'department name is Engineering'. For any row in the DEPARTMENTS table, this predicate is either true or false. The department name is either 'Engineering' or it is not. Now let's use this predicate in the WHERE clause of a SELECT statement:

```
SELECT *
FROM DEPARTMENTS
WHERE DEPT_NAME = 'Engineering'  ;
```

DEPT_NO	DEPT_NAME	HEAD	BUDGET	P_BUDGET
1	Engineering	59	5780000	6200000

Notice that the word Engineering is in single quotes. These must be used to specify all text strings. This query retrieves all the rows in the DEPARTMENTS table where the DEPT_NAME is Engineering. In this case, it retrieves only one record. In this query, we have used the asterisk to retrieve all the columns from DEPARTMENTS in the results. You do not have to include the columns that appear in the WHERE clause in the results, but it helps to highlight what the query is doing.

When processing a query with a predicate, the DBMS goes through all the rows in the table and checks to see if the predicate is true or false for each row. This is the type of query which is greatly speeded up if the row that is used in the predicate is indexed.

Comparison Operator	Relation	Example of use
=	Equals to	surname = 'Jones'
<	Less than	mark < 65
>	Greater than	salary > 45000
<=	Equal to or less than	surname <= 'Smith'
>=	Equal to or greater than	date >= 12-Aug-1993
<>	Not equal to	dept_no <> 14

Figure 4.2 Comparison operators used in SQL predicates

4.2.1 Comparison Test Operators: =, <, <=, >, >=, <>

In the previous section we saw how predicates evaluate equivalence statements as either true or false. As well as the equals to operator, (=), SQL also allows you to use the other comparison operators shown in Figure 4.2. The predicate resolves to either true or false for each row in the table for all these comparison operators as well. For example, let's run a query that gets the names of all those lecturers who earn more than 60,000:

```
SELECT INITL, SURNAME
   FROM LECTURERS
   WHERE PAY > 60000;
```

INITL	SURNAME
W M	Nizamuddin

The operators shown in Figure 4.2 are standard mathematical signs that act on numerical information. In SQL predicates, they can also be applied to character type values. The result of the predicate will depend on the character representation system used by the computer's operating system. Most microcomputer and minicomputer systems use the ASCII system. Some large mainframes use a system known as EBCDIC. Both these systems represent alphanumeric characters as numeric values that the computer can understand. SQL uses these underlying numeric values as the basis of comparison. In this book, we will assume that all the examples we use are run on an ASCII system. As this is the most popular system, this is quite a good assumption. Let's look at an example. In the STUDENTS table, to list the names of all the students whose surname begins with characters from M to Z:

```
SELECT SURNAME, FIRST_NAME
   FROM STUDENTS
   WHERE SURNAME > 'M' ;
```

SURNAME	FIRST_NAME
Patel	Mahesh
Scott	Gavin T J
Monkhouse	Robert Jones
Middleton	Jane P
Mulla	Farook F U
Wickes	Wendy Y Y W

SQL Tips

> The ANSI/ISO standard specifies the inequality operator as <>.
> IBM's DB2 and SQL/DS use ¬= and SQL Server uses !=.

Notice that the rows are not arranged in alphabetical order. SQL lists the rows in the order in which it finds them in the table. Ordering is possible in SELECT, and this will be discussed in later sections of this chapter.

In the previous query, we used the uppercase character, M, in the predicate. It is important to remember that M is not the same as m. If we had used the lowercase character instead, SQL would not have found any matching records:

```
SELECT SURNAME, FIRST_NAME
   FROM STUDENTS
   WHERE SURNAME > 'm' ;
```

No matching records found.

The reason for this query coming up empty is that in the ASCII scheme, uppercase characters are defined as being less (they have a lower underlying numeric value) than lowercase characters. All the surnames in the STUDENTS table start with an uppercase letter and so in the ASCII scheme, they are all less than the lowercase m. The values assigned in ASCII are reversed in EBCDIC, so lowercase characters are less than uppercase. You need to be sure which scheme your computer system uses before constructing your queries.

4.2.2 Range Test Operator: BETWEEN

The BETWEEN range test operator allows you to define a predicate in the form of a range. If a column value for a row falls within this range, then the predicate is true and the row will be added to the results table. The BETWEEN range test consists of two keywords, BETWEEN and AND. It must be supplied with the upper and the lower range values. The first value must be the lower bound and the second value, the upper bound. For example, in the LECTURERS table, if we wanted to look at the records of all those lecturers who earn between 31,800 and 40,900:

```
SELECT SURNAME, PAY
   FROM LECTURERS
   WHERE PAY BETWEEN 31800 AND 40900 ;
```

SURNAME	PAY
Scrivens	31800
Ramanujan	40900
Finley	34210

This query retrieves three records. Notice that the upper and lower parameters are inclusive. This means that the rows where pay equals 31,800 (lower bound) and 40,900 (upper bound) are also retrieved in the results. SQL will not allow you to specify the upper bound first. Thus the following query does not return any records:

```
SELECT SURNAME, PAY
  FROM LECTURERS
  WHERE PAY BETWEEN 40900 AND 31800 ;
```

No matching records found.

You can use character values as upper and lower range bounds:

```
SELECT *
  FROM LECTURERS
  WHERE SURNAME BETWEEN 'N' AND 'R' ;
```

SURNAME	INITL	LECT_NO	DEPT_NO	SUB_NO	GRADE	PAY	JOINED
Nizamuddin	W M	3	3	4	A	86790	05-26-1969

The query only retrieves one row because Nizamuddin is between N and R, but Ramanujan is not. When comparing strings of unequal length, SQL pads out the smaller string with spaces before doing the comparison. As the space character has a lower value than letter characters in the ASCII scheme, the word Ramanujan falls outside the upper bound.

BETWEEN does not actually add any new functionality to SQL. All queries that use BETWEEN can be rephrased to run using only the comparison test operators instead. For example the last query can be expressed without using BETWEEN as:

```
SELECT *
  FROM LECTURERS
  WHERE (SURNAME >= 'N') AND (SURNAME <= 'R') ;
```

SURNAME	INITL	LECT_NO	DEPT_NO	SUB_NO	GRADE	PAY	JOINED
Nizamuddin	W M	3	3	4	A	86790	05-26-1969

The AND keyword is a boolean operator that tells SQL that both expressions inside the parentheses must be true for the predicate to be true. Although this query is functionally the same as the previous query, the one using BETWEEN is more elegant and it is clearer to the reader what the query is trying to achieve.

4.2.3 Set Membership Test Operator: IN

We've seen that BETWEEN defines a range of values to check against for inclusion or exclusion from the results table. This is not always enough. What if you needed to check for certain values only? Values that do not always fit into a neat range. To accommodate this, SQL allows the use of the IN operator. An example will illustrate the use of IN. In the SUBJECTS table, if we wanted to look at the rows of the Anatomy and the Physiology subjects, we could use a query with IN:

```
SELECT *
  FROM SUBJECTS
  WHERE SUB_NAME IN ('Anatomy', 'Physiology') ;
```

SUB_NO	SUB_NAME	DEPT_NO	CREDITS	PASS
7	Physiology	6	3	78
8	Anatomy	6	1	74

You must define the set values within parentheses, and must separate each value with a comma. In this example, we have used string values. IN also allows other valid data types to be used as set members for example to list the subjects rows given that their pass marks are 52, 56 and 57:

```
SELECT SUB_NAME, PASS
  FROM SUBJECTS
  WHERE PASS IN (52, 56, 57) ;
```

SUB_NAME	PASS
Industrial Law	52
Organic Chemistry	57
Marketing	56

As with all the SQL query commands, the result records are not displayed in any order unless the ordering is explicitly specified. In the above query for example, we specified pass marks of 52, 56 and 57 in the inclusion set. The results table displayed the rows in the 52, 57, 56 order. The reason for this is that this is the order in which the DBMS found the rows in the table.

As with BETWEEN, IN does not add to SQL's functionality. What IN does can also be accomplished by using comparison and boolean operators. For example, the previous query can also be expressed as:

```
SELECT SUB_NAME, PASS
   FROM SUBJECTS
   WHERE PASS = 52
      OR PASS = 56
      OR PASS = 57 ;
```

SUB_NAME	PASS
Industrial Law	52
Organic Chemistry	57
Marketing	56

4.2.4 Pattern Matching Test Operator: LIKE

The LIKE operator is used to match string pattern values. LIKE uses wildcard characters to specify one or more string character values. ANSI/ISO SQL defines two wildcard characters, the underscore (_) and the percent (%). These are the characters that are almost universally used in commercial SQL systems for pattern matching. String pattern matching is useful in cases where you are not sure of the exact string value that you need to search for. For example if you cannot remember the spelling of a person's name:

```
SELECT *
   FROM STUDENTS
   WHERE SURNAME LIKE 'A_ton';
```

SURNAME	FIRST_NAME	D_O_B	STUDENT_NO	DEPT_NO	YEAR
Ayton	Phil J M A	07-13-1967	3	3	1

The underscore character is one of the wildcards, and is used to represent any valid character (one only). In this query, we are not sure if the student's surname is spelt as Ayton or Aeton or even Aiton. The LIKE 'A_ton' predicate tells SQL that the first letter of the surname is 'A' and the last three letters are 'ton', but we are not sure of the second letter. If you are familiar with the MS-DOS or OS/2 or UNIX operating systems, then the _ character performs the same function in SQL as ? does in MS-DOS, and . does in UNIX.

The previous query told SQL to retrieve those rows where the second letter of the surname is any valid character. The rest of the pattern i.e. the first and the last three letters must match exactly as specified.

The second wildcard character you can use in LIKE is the percent (%) character. This is used to represent a sequence of zero or more characters. The percent wildcard in SQL corresponds to the * wildcard in MS-DOS and OS/2 and UNIX. Let's use percent to look at the records of all those students whose surname ends in 'ton':

```
SELECT *
  FROM STUDENTS
  WHERE SURNAME LIKE '%ton' ;
```

SURNAME	FIRST_NAME	D_O_B	STUDENT_NO	DEPT_NO	YEAR
Ayton	Phil J M A	07-13-1967	3	3	1

You can also mix and match the % and the _ wildcard characters in a single query:

```
SELECT *
  FROM STUDENTS
  WHERE SURNAME LIKE 'A_t%' ;
```

SURNAME	FIRST_NAME	D_O_B	STUDENT_NO	DEPT_NO	YEAR
Ayton	Phil J M A	07-13-1967	3	3	1

The % and _ characters are themselves legal ASCII characters. Using valid characters as wildcards can cause problems. What if you wanted to use % or _ as part of the string and not as wildcards? SQL's solution to this is to allow you to define and use the escape character. The escape character has a special meaning in the LIKE string in that the character immediately following it is treated as a regular character and not a wildcard. For example suppose we wanted to search for the string '_search%' where % and _ are regular characters and not wildcards, then we could use the following query with the ESCAPE clause:

```
SELECT *
  FROM SUBJECTS
  WHERE SUB_NAME LIKE '$_SEARCH$%' ESCAPE '$' ;
```

No matching records found.

The ESCAPE clause at the end of the query defines the dollar ($) character as the escape character. In the string, '$_search$%', % and _ are treated as characters and not as wildcards. Of course, this query comes up empty because we do not have a subject called '%search_' in the SUBJECTS table.

SQL Tips

> IBM's DB2, OS/2 Extended Edition, Oracle and SQL Server do not support the ESCAPE clause.

4.2.5 NULL Value Test Operator: IS NULL

As we know NULL values are used to indicate that no data has been defined yet. This is different from blank string values or zero numeric values. Blank and zero values are just that, values. NULL marks the column as not having any definite value. When you use NULLs in SQL expressions, the result will always be undefined. For example, if you wanted to look at the rows in the LECTURERS table where the value for the DEPT_NO field is NULL, the following query will not retrieve the results you want:

```
SELECT SURNAME, DEPT_NO
  FROM LECTURERS
  WHERE DEPT_NO = NULL ;
```

SURNAME	DEPT_NO
Jones	1
Scrivens	3
Nizamuddin	3
Campbell	5
Ramanujan	4
Finley	4

The DBMS retrieved all the lecturers row in our system because the predicate "DEPT_NO = NULL" is unknown for all the rows. It is neither true nor false. Another DBMS could just as easily have not retrieved any rows depending upon how it treats unknown predicate results. SQL provides the IS NULL operator to search specifically for NULL values. The valid form of the previous query is thus:

```
SELECT SURNAME, DEPT_NO
  FROM LECTURERS
  WHERE DEPT_NO IS NULL ;
```

No matching records found.

The NOT logical operator (discussed in the next section) can be used to reverse the meaning of IS NULL. To retrieve the rows of those lecturers where the DEPT_NO value is not NULL:

```
SELECT SURNAME,  DEPT_NO
  FROM LECTURERS
  WHERE DEPT_NO IS NULL ;
```

SURNAME	DEPT_NO
Jones	1
Scrivens	3
Nizamuddin	3
Campbell	5
Ramanujan	4
Finley	4

NOT can also be used with the other operators, e.g. NOT BETWEEN and NOT LIKE to reverse their meaning.

4.2.6 Logical Operators: AND, OR and NOT

The scope of the WHERE clause and the operators used with it can be extended by using the logical operators AND, OR and NOT. They enable you to specify compound search conditions to fine tune your data retrieval requirements. The functioning of these operators is shown in Figure 4.3. The logical operators link multiple predicates within a single WHERE clause. For example, to see the records of those subjects which have a credit value of 1 and whose pass mark value is greater than 70%, we need two predicates in the WHERE clause:

```
SELECT SUB_NAME
  FROM SUBJECTS
  WHERE CREDITS = 1
    AND PASS > 70 ;
```

```
SUB_NAME
————————————————

Engineering Drwg
Anatomy
```

The WHERE evaluates to true if both the first predicate (CREDITS = 1) AND the second predicate (PASS > 70) are true. As with the single predicate query, the DBMS processes all the rows in the STUDENTS table one by one and checks to see if this multiple predicate evaluates to true or false for each row. You can use as many logical operators as you like to link predicates into complex expressions:

```
SELECT * FROM LECTURERS
  WHERE DEPT_NO = 4
    AND (GRADE > 'C' OR PAY <= 30000)
    AND NOT LECT_NO = 5 ;
```

Logical Operator	Usage	Result
AND	Predicate 1 AND Predicate 2	Returns true if both Predicate 1 and Predicate 2 are true.
OR	Predicate 1 OR Predicate 2	Returns true if either Predicate 1 or Predicate 2 are true.
NOT	NOT Boolean Expression 1	Returns true if Expression 1 is false. Returns false if Expression 1 is true.

Figure 4.3   Logical operators used in SQL

SURNAME	INITL	LECT_NO	DEPT_NO	SUB_NO	GRADE	PAY	JOINED
Finley	G Y	6	4	5	D	34210	03-28-1960

SQL lets you group expressions by using parentheses. These have the same effect in SQL expressions as they do in mathematical expressions. The expressions inside the parenthesis are evaluated first, and are treated as a single expression. In the previous query, AND applies to the expression inside the parenthesis as a whole, i.e. GRADE > 'C' OR PAY <= 30000. When you are analyzing complex WHERE clauses, it is best to break the WHERE into its constituent predicates and reading them in plain English. Let's apply this to the last query. The first search condition is "department number is equal to 4". The AND links this to a parenthesized expression, "either the grade is lower than C or pay is 30,000 or less". You need to be careful here because grade D is lower than grade C but the character D is greater than C. The last predicate is slightly more tricky. In English, we would say "lecturer number is not equal to 5". SQL doesn't let you construct this as LECT_NO NOT = 5. The NOT must precede the boolean expression that it operates on. If we now put these all together, the WHERE clause can be expressed as "Where department number is equal to 4 and either the grade is lower than C or pay is 30,000 or less and also, the lecturer number is not equal to 5".

SQL Tips

> The ANSI/ISO standard specifies that NOT has the highest precedence, followed by AND and then OR.

4.3 Ordering the output of a query: The ORDER BY clause

In all the queries we've seen so far, the rows in the results table have not been ordered in any way. SQL just retrieved the rows in the order in which it found them in the table. The ORDER BY clause allows you to impose an order on the query results.

You can use ORDER BY with one or more column names to specify the ordering of the query results. For example, to list students' records in alphabetical order by surname:

```
SELECT *
  FROM STUDENTS
  ORDER BY SURNAME ;
```

SURNAME	FIRST_NAME	D_O_B	STUDENT_NO	DEPT_NO	YEAR
Al-Eassawy	Zaid M A	11-26-1970	2	4	2
Ayton	Phil J M A	07-13-1967	3	3	1
Baker	Abu-Mia	03-13-1971	7	4	1
Brown	Joseph P A	04-19-1970	8	3	3
Duke	Fitzroy	11-26-1970	1	4	2
Grimm	Hans Johan	06-21-1971	10	2	1
Gyver	Sue L J V	07-30-1968	11	4	2
Hung-Sun	Jimmy Lau	08-11-1969	12	1	3
Jones	Gareth P Y	01-24-1970	5	2	1
Layton	Hugh	11-16-1971	15	5	1
Middleton	Jane P	09-14-1971	13	1	3
Monkhouse	Robert Jones	05-23-1967	9	1	1
Mulla	Farook F U	10-24-1968	14	3	2
Patel	Mahesh	12-07-1970	4	2	1
Scott	Gavin T J	02-20-1971	6	2	2

The ORDER BY clause only affects the manner in which these rows are displayed by SQL. It does not have any effect on the order in which the records are stored on disk. If there are NULL values in the ORDER BY column then they appear either at the beginning or at the end of the list depending on your dialect of SQL.

This query listed the student's rows alphabetically by SURNAME, in ascending order. This is the default. We can explicitly specify the ordering by using the ASC (for ascending) and the DESC (for descending) keywords. If we had used DESC in the previous query:

```
SELECT *
  FROM STUDENTS
  ORDER BY SURNAME DESC ;
```

SURNAME	FIRST_NAME	D_O_B	STUDENT_NO	DEPT_NO	YEAR
Wickes	Wendy Y Y W	12-05-1969	16	1	1
Scott	Gavin T J	02-20-1971	6	2	2
Patel	Mahesh	12-07-1970	4	2	1
Mulla	Farook F U	10-24-1968	14	3	2
Monkhouse	Robert Jones	05-23-1967	9	1	1
Middleton	Jane P	09-14-1971	13	1	3
Layton	Hugh	11-16-1971	15	5	1
Jones	Gareth P Y	01-24-1970	5	2	1
Hung-Sun	Jimmy Lau	08-11-1969	12	1	3
Gyver	Sue L J V	07-30-1968	11	4	2
Grimm	Hans Johan	06-21-1971	10	2	1
Duke	Fitzroy	11-26-1970	1	4	2
Brown	Joseph P A	04-19-1970	8	3	3
Baker	Abu-Mia	03-13-1971	7	4	1
Ayton	Phil J M A	07-13-1967	3	3	1

The students are now listed in reverse alphabetical order. Note that ASC is optional. If neither DESC OR ASC is specified then ASC is assumed to be in effect.

You can use ORDER BY with more than one column. In this case, SQL will use the first column as the primary ordering field, the second column as the secondary and so on. In our STUDENTS table for example, to list the students' records by departments and within each department by surname:

```
SELECT *
  FROM STUDENTS
  ORDER BY DEPT_NO, SURNAME ;
```

SURNAME	FIRST_NAME	D_O_B	STUDENT_NO	DEPT_NO	YEAR
Hung-Sun	Jimmy Lau	08-11-1969	12	1	3
Middleton	Jane P	09-14-1971	13	1	3
Monkhouse	Robert Jones	05-23-1967	9	1	1
Wickes	Wendy Y Y W	12-05-1969	16	1	1
Grimm	Hans Johan	06-21-1971	10	2	1
Jones	Gareth P Y	01-24-1970	5	2	1
Patel	Mahesh	12-07-1970	4	2	1
Scott	Gavin T J	02-20-1971	6	2	2
Ayton	Phil J M A	07-13-1967	3	3	1
Brown	Joseph P A	04-19-1970	8	3	3
Mulla	Farook F U	10-24-1968	14	3	2
Al-Eassawy	Zaid M A	11-26-1970	2	4	2
Baker	Abu-Mia	03-13-1971	7	4	1
Duke	Fitzroy	11-26-1970	1	4	2
Gyver	Sue L J V	07-30-1968	11	4	2

Notice that the rows in the results table are now ordered by the DEPT_NO field. This is the primary ordering field. Within each department, the students are displayed in alphabetical order by SURNAME. This is the secondary ordering field. Although you can use as many ordering fields as you like in the ORDER BY clause, the ANSI/ISO standard requires that the columns used in the ORDER BY clause are also displayed in the results table. This means that they must be specified in the SELECT clause, either explicitly by name, or implicitly by using the asterisk. This ANSI/ISO requirement is not enforced by all SQL dialects but it is a good idea to adhere to it anyway for portability reasons.

You have seen how to order results rows by using column names in the ORDER BY clause. What if you don't know what the column name is?

Such situations are not as remote as you might think. For example calculated columns and aggregate functions cannot be referred to by their column name. To overcome this, ORDER BY also accepts column number values. For example, we can list the contents of the DEPARTMENTS table in allocated budget order either by specifying ORDER BY BUDGET or by specifying the column number:

```
SELECT DEPT_NO, DEPT_NAME, BUDGET
  FROM DEPARTMENTS
  ORDER BY 3 ;
```

DEPT_NO	DEPT_NAME	BUDGET
6	Medicine	6895000
1	Engineering	5780000
5	Physical Sciences	4680000
3	Management Studies	2510000
2	Arts & Humanities	753000
4	Industrial Law	78000

The first column specified in the SELECT clause is always column 1. Subsequent columns have numeric values according to where they are specified in SELECT and not where they occur in the table itself. This applies to calculated columns as well:

```
SELECT DEPT_NAME, (BUDGET * 2.25)
  FROM DEPARTMENTS
  ORDER BY 2 ;
```

DEPT_NAME	
Medicine	775687500
Physical Sciences	526500000
Industrial Law	877500
Management Studies	28237500
Arts & Humanities	8471250
Engineering	65025000

4.4   Summary of data in tables: The ANSI aggregate functions

The rows in a table are elemental pieces of information that you can use to base your decisions on. Very often, the data that you need can be found directly in one or more columns. But sometimes, the data is based on the values of all the rows in the table. For example, if you need to know the average mark in the exams table, you must add up the marks for all the students, then divide that value by the number of students in the table. ANSI/ISO SQL provides five functions, known as aggregate functions which can be used to summarize data in tables. These functions operate on the table data and produce a single value as output.

The five ANSI/ISO functions are:

COUNT( )   outputs the number of rows or column values that would be selected by the query. The function does not actually list any of the rows, but only a value denoting the total number of rows or column values that the query retrieves.

SUM( )   outputs the sum total of all the column values that are addressed by the query. This function can only be used with numeric type columns.

AVG( )   outputs the average (arithmetic mean) of the column values addressed by the query. As with the SUM( ) function, AVG( ) can only be used with numeric type columns.

MIN( )   outputs the minimum, the smallest, column value from those that are addressed by the query.

MAX( )   outputs the maximum, the largest, column value from those that are addressed by the query.

Aggregate functions can be used in the select list just like regular columns with the following provisions: You cannot nest aggregate functions and you cannot mix regular columns and aggregate functions in the same query.

4.4.1 The number of values or rows: The COUNT( ) function

There are two different versions of the COUNT( ) aggregate function that ANSI/ISO allows. The first counts and lists the number of non-NULL values in a particular column. The second counts and displays the total number of rows that would be retrieved by a query. These two versions of COUNT( ) differ only in the arguments that are passed to them.

Let's use COUNT( ) to count the number of data values in a column. To find out how many students have been assigned to a department in the STUDENTS table:

```
SELECT COUNT(DEPT_NO)
  FROM STUDENTS;
```

COUNT(DEPT_NO)

————————————
             16

In our case, all the students are assigned a department number and the number output by the query is the same as the number of students there are in the table. If this were not the case, i.e. if there were NULL values in the DEPT_NO field for some of the student's rows, then these rows would not appear in the COUNT( ) function's total.

To count the number of different values in a column, the column name must be preceded by the DISTINCT keyword. For example, to look at the number of different departments that are represented in the DEPT_NO field of the STUDENTS table:

```
SELECT COUNT(DISTINCT DEPT_NO)
  FROM STUDENTS;
```

COUNT(DEPT_NO)

————————————
            5

The output from this query is 5 because there are five different department number values in this column. The ANSI/ISO standard states that DISTINCT must be used with column names in the COUNT( ) function, most commercial versions of SQL relax this requirement and leave it up to the user to use DISTINCT or not.

As pointed out earlier, the COUNT( ) function can also be used to count rows in a table as well as column values. To do this, COUNT( ) must be used with an asterisk. To count the number of rows in the EXAMS table:

```
SELECT COUNT(*)
  FROM EXAMS;
```

COUNT(*)

————————
    19

The COUNT(*) total includes all the rows addressed by the query, including NULL and duplicate rows. If we are only interested in knowing the number of exams taken by a particular student, we would have to use the WHERE clause to retrieve those rows that we are interested in:

```
SELECT COUNT(*)
  FROM EXAMS
  WHERE STUDENT_NO = 1 ;
```

```
COUNT(*)
--------
    3
```

4.4.2 The total of values: The SUM( ) function

The SUM( ) aggregate function calculates the sum total of the values in a column. The parameter passed to SUM( ) must be the name of the column either by itself or used in a scalar expression. The data in the columns used by SUM( ) must be of numeric type such as integer, decimal, etc. Let's use SUM( ) to find the total expenditure on staff pay:

```
SELECT SUM(PAY)
  FROM LECTURERS  ;
```

```
SUM(PAY)
--------
 261270
```

This query adds up all the values in the PAY column and lists the final total. The output of SUM( ) (and also the other aggregate functions that deal with numeric type data) is usually of the same data type as the column data but sometimes, the result is of greater precision than the column data.

You can use scalar expressions as parameters to the aggregate functions. The following query adds 1500 to each lecturer's pay and calculates the sum total:

```
SELECT SUM(PAY), SUM(PAY + 1500)
  FROM LECTURERS ;
```

```
SUM(PAY)         SUM(PAY+1500)
--------         -------------
 261270              270270
```

In this simple example, we could have calculated this value by adding 1500 x 6 = 9000 to the SUM(PAY) value. Scalar expressions are most useful when you want to look at say, the total expenditure on pay for a percentage increase in salary for each lecturer. For example, this query finds the total expenditure on pay if we increase each lecturer's salary by 7.5%:

```
SELECT SUM(PAY), SUM(PAY * 1.075)
  FROM LECTURERS ;
```

SUM(PAY)	SUM(PAY*1.075)
261270	280865

4.4.3 The average value: The AVG( ) function

The AVG( ) function calculates the average or arithmetic mean of the values in a column. AVG( ) can only be applied to numeric type columns and outputs a numeric value. SQL calculates the average by adding up all the values in the column, then dividing the total by the number of values. As an example, the following query calculates the average pay for a lecturer:

```
SELECT AVG(PAY)
  FROM LECTURERS  ;
```

AVG(PAY)
43545

We can also selectively calculate averages. This query finds the average mark obtained by students in a particular subject:

```
SELECT AVG(MARK)
  FROM EXAMS
  WHERE SUB_NO = 5 ;
```

AVG MARK
55

4.4.4 The minimum and maximum values: The MIN( ) and MAX( ) functions

The MIN( ) function finds the smallest value in a column of data. MIN( ) can operate on string and numeric data types as well as non-ANSI types such as date and time. For example, to find the earliest date when a lecturer joined the staff:

SELECT MIN(JOINED)
  FROM LECTURERS ;

MIN(JOINED)
–––––––––––––
03-28-1960

SQL Tips

> In the EBCDIC character set, which is used in IBM mainframes, the lowercase characters precede the uppercase characters which precede digits.

Most dialects of SQL treat earlier dates and times as being less than later dates and times. So to find the last date when a lecturer joined the staff:

SELECT MAX(JOINED)
FROM LECTURERS ;

MAX(JOINED)
–––––––––––––
03-25-1990

MIN( ) and MAX( ) both allow you to use scalar expressions as well as column names as parameters. For example, if the average pass mark for all subjects was found to be 58%, then this query finds the lowest difference in percentage points between this mark and the exam marks:

SELECT MIN(58 - MARK)
FROM EXAMS ;

MIN(58 - MARK)
–––––––––––––
    −31

The query comes up with the answer of -31 because the highest mark in EXAMS is 89 and 58 - 89 = -31. This result may not be what you expected and serves to illustrate an important point. You need to be careful when wording your queries to ensure that they do what you intend them to do.

The order of precedence within the data types is shown in Figure 4.4. Remember that this applies only to the ASCII character scheme.

	DATES	NUMERIC	STRING
	01-JAN-1980	-100.50	123ABC
	31-JAN-1980	0.40	ABCDEF
	01-DEC-1980	0	Abcdef
DECREASE	01-JAN-1981	250.30	abcdef

Figure 4.4   Order of precedence within data types

SQL Tips

> The ANSI/ISO standard specifies that NULL values are ignored by the column functions.

4.4.5 Sub-totals of values: The GROUP BY clause

The aggregate functions described in the previous section have been used to produce grand totals. Values output by them are just like the totals that appear at the end of each column listing in a report. You can also use these functions to output sub-total values. The GROUP BY clause of the SELECT statement lets you split up the values in a column into subsets. The aggregate functions are then applied to these subsets instead of the column as a whole. For example, in the EXAMS table, we could find the average mark obtained by the students by:

```
SELECT AVG(MARK)
  FROM EXAMS ;
```

AVG(MARK)
‾‾‾‾‾‾‾‾‾‾
55

SQL Tips

> SQL Server allows the COMPUTE clauser which is used to calculate subtotals of subtotals.

This value is not very informative as the exams were sat by students of all abilities. It would be more meaningful to get the average mark for each student. This can be obtained by using the GROUP BY clause:

SELECT STUDENT_NO, AVG(MARK)
    FROM EXAMS
    GROUP BY STUDENT_NO ;

STUDENT_NO	AVG(MARK)
1	62
2	52
3	70
4	42
5	55
6	74
7	45
8	62

This query first groups the rows in the EXAMS table by the values in STUDENT_NO. The AVG( ) function then operates on each group. The average values output are thus the averages for the exams taken by individual students.

Queries using the GROUP BY clause are known as grouped queries. All the rules for using the ANSI/ISO functions that we have looked at also apply to grouped queries. The only difference being that in grouped queries, the DBMS applies the functions to each group individually rather than to the column as a whole. You can also get the same results by running several queries with a WHERE clause. For example, to find the average mark for a student:

```
SELECT STUDENT_NO, AVG(MARK)
  FROM EXAMS
  WHERE STUDENT_NO = 1 ;
```

STUDENT_NO	AVG(MARK)
1	65

By changing the 1 value in the predicate, we could calculate the average for different students.

GROUP BY can be used with multiple fields. For example, in the SUBJECTS table, to find the highest pass mark for each department/credits combination:

```
SELECT SUB_NAME, DEPT_NO, CREDITS, MAX(PASS)
  FROM SUBJECTS
  GROUP BY DEPT_NO, CREDITS ;
```

SUB_NAME	DEPT_NO	CREDITS	MAX(PASS)
Engineering Drwg	1	1	71
Mathematics	1	2	65
Electronics	1	3	71
English Lit	2	1	60
Basic Accounts	3	1	67
Marketing	3	2	56
Industrial Law	4	2	52
Organic Chemistry	5	3	57
Anatomy	6	3	78
Physiology	6	3	78

SQL Tips

> SQL Server's COMPUTE clause produces non-table results which are, needless to say, highly non-standard.

4.4.6 Eliminating groups of data: The HAVING clause

You cannot use aggregate functions in the WHERE clause of a SELECT statement. This means that you cannot use WHERE to selectively eliminate data that does not interest you from the results of aggregate queries. For example, in the query that we used to find the average mark for each student, if we are only interested in averages that are above 56%, then SQL won't let you use the following query because it uses AVG( ) in the WHERE clause:

```
SELECT STUDENT_NO, AVG(MARK)
   FROM EXAMS
   WHERE AVG(MARK) > 56
   GROUP BY STUDENT_NO ;
```

Error 67: Aggregate function used in WHERE.

The HAVING clause performs a similar function to WHERE in that it eliminates groups from the results table. Thus to list only those students where the average is above 56%:

```
SELECT STUDENT_NO, AVG(MARK)
   FROM EXAMS
   GROUP BY STUDENT_NO
   HAVING AVG(MARK) > 56 ;
```

STUDENT_NO	AVG(MARK)
1	62
3	70
6	74
8	62

The field referenced by HAVING can not have more than one value for each group. This means that in practice HAVING can only reference aggregate functions and columns that are used in GROUP BY.

4.5   Retrieving data from multiple tables: SQL joins

So far, we've been looking at queries that retrieve data from a single table at a time. Single table queries are useful but they do not exploit the full power of the SQL language. SQL is a relational database query language and as such, one of its most important features is its ability to retrieve information from several different related tables. In relational database terms, this process is called a join. The tables to be joined are named in the FROM clause of the SELECT with each table name separated by a comma. The relationships between the tables in a join are defined by the predicate in the WHERE clause. The predicate can refer to any column from the joined tables to form the relations. For example, to list the names of all the lecturers and the subjects that they teach:

```
SELECT LECTURERS.SURNAME, SUBJECTS.SUB_NAME
   FROM LECTURERS, SUBJECTS
   WHERE LECTURERS.DEPT_NO = SUBJECTS.DEPT_NO ;
```

LECTURERS.SURNAME	SUBJECTS.SUB_NAME
Jones	Electronics
Jones	Engineering Drawing
Jones	Mathematics
Scrivens	Marketing
Scrivens	Basic Accounts
Nizamuddin	Marketing
Nizamuddin	Basic Accounts
Campbell	Organic Chemistry
Ramanujan	Industrial Law
Finley	Industrial Law

Of course, this join assumes that all the lecturers are multi-skilled in that each is able to teach all the subjects in one particular department. Notice the column naming convention we have used. The column names in this query are prefixed by the name of the table that the column is part of. If all the columns in the joined tables had unique names, then the table prefix would not have been required. In our university example though, there is a column called DEPT_NO in both the LECTURERS and the SUBJECTS tables. In this case we must use LECTURERS.DEPT_NO and SUBJECTS.DEPT_NO to distinguish between the columns. Generally, it is good to get into the habit of using the table name prefix to specify columns. As your queries get more and more complex, it may not always be clear to the reader which column you mean if the table prefix is not used.

In the last query we did not have to tell SQL how to retrieve the data from the tables, instead, we merely specified what data we wanted to see. The actual tables themselves might have been stored on disks located at different sites. SQL shields the user from these technicalities in that you do not have to know how to get at the data or even where it is. You only have to specify the data to get at. When processing a query with a join, SQL looks at all the possible combination of rows from the tables in the join and uses the criteria defined in the predicate to add or omit the rows from the results table. The steps involved in processing this query are shown in Figure 4.5.

We saw in the simple query, how we can use the asterisk character to mean "all the columns". This also applies to queries involving table joins. The following query lists all the columns of the joined tables:

```
SELECT *
  FROM LECTURERS, SUBJECTS
  WHERE LECTURERS.DEPT_NO = SUBJECTS.DEPT_NO ;
```

SURNAME	INITL	LECT_NO	DEPT_NO	SUB_NO	GRADE	PAY	JOINED
Jones	R A	1	1	2	E	24000	03-25-1990
Jones	R A	1	1	2	E	24000	03-25-1990
Jones	R A	1	1	2	E	24000	03-25-1990
Scrivens	T R	2	3	1	D	31800	09-30-1986
Scrivens	T R	2	3	1	D	31800	09-30-1986
Nizamuddin	W M	3	3	4	A	86790	05-26-1969
Nizamuddin	W M	3	3	4	A	86790	05-26-1969
Campbell	J G	4	5	3	C	43570	02-23-1980
Ramanujan	S	5	4	5	C	40900	01-01-1985

The asterisk causes all the columns of both joined tables to be listed but since the screen is only 80 columns wide, only those columns that fit on the screen are shown in the above example. The asterisk is not usually used as it retrieves too much irrelevant information. When joining tables, we are only interested in columns that convey useful information that is directly related to the query.

The last query established a join between the LECTURERS table and the SUBJECTS table through the use of columns which have the same data type in both tables, i.e. the LECTURERS.DEPT_NO and the

SURNAME	SUB NAME	
Jones	Mathematics	————> Add to Results
Jones	English Lit	
Jones	Engineering Drwg	——> Add to Results
Jones	Basic Accounts	
. .	. .	
. .	. .	
Jones	Electronics	————> Add to Results
Jones	Marketing	
Scrivens	Mathematics	
Scrivens	English Lit	
. .	. .	
. .	. .	
Scrivens	Marketing	————> Add to Results
. .	. .	
. .	. .	
Finley	Marketing	

————————> = The predicate is true for this row combination.

1. Construct a list of every possible combination of rows from the LECTURERS and the SUBJECTS table.

2. Check to see if the predicate is true for each combination of rows, i.e. if LECTURERS. DEPT_NO = SUBJECTS. DEPT_NO.

3. If the predicate is true, then add the LECTURERS.SURNAME and the SUBJECTS.SUB_NAME value for the row to the results table.

4. When all the combination rows have been checked, display the results table.

Figure 4.5   Processing a query with a two table join

SUBJECTS.DEPT_NO columns. In relational databases, certain linkages are defined when the tables are first created, the primary key/foreign key relationships for example. Joins can easily use these 'natural' relationships to extract data from tables. For example, the DEPT_NO column is the primary key in the DEPARTMENTS table and a foreign key in the SUBJECTS table which refers to DEPARTMENTS. So we can join these two tables using this column:

```
SELECT SUBJECTS.SUB_NAME, DEPARTMENTS.DEPT_NAME
   FROM SUBJECTS, DEPARTMENTS
   WHERE SUBJECTS.DEPT_NO = DEPARTMENTS.DEPT_NO ;
```

SUBJECTS.SUB_NAME	DEPARTMENTS.DEPT_NAME
Mathematics	Engineering
English Lit	Arts & Humanities
Engineering Drwg	Engineering
Basic Accounts	Management Studies
Industrial Law	Industrial Law
Organic Chemistry	Physical Sciences
Physiology	Medicine
Anatomy	Medicine
Electronics	Engineering
Marketing	Management Studies

Each subject is listed along with the department that offers it. Notice that we did not specify the DEPT_NO field in the SELECT list. We only used DEPT_NO in the predicate to form a link between the two tables. In practice, primary and foreign key columns seldom appear in the results table because they are often just sequential numbers or a combination of numbers and letters that do not mean very much to the reader. The associated columns in the record that the key identifies convey far more information e.g. the SURNAME, DEPT_NAME, BUDGET, etc.

You can also extend the join to more than two tables. For example, If we modify the previous query to include the names of the lecturers that teach the course, we would be joining three tables:

```
SELECT   SUBJECTS.SUB_NAME,  DEPARTMENTS.DEPT_NAME
LECTURERS.SURNAME
   FROM SUBJECTS, DEPARTMENTS, LECTURERS
   WHERE SUBJECTS.DEPT_NO = DEPARTMENTS.DEPT_NO ;
```

SUBJECTS.SUB_NAME	DEPARTMENTS.DEPT_NAME	LECTURERS.SURNAME
Mathematics	Engineering	Jones
English Lit	Arts & Humanities	Jones
Engineering Drwg	Engineering	Nizamuddin
Basic Accounts	Management Studies	Scrivens
Industrial Law	Industrial Law	Finley
Organic Chemistry	Physical Sciences	Ramanujan
Physiology	Medicine	Campbell
Anatomy	Medicine	Jones
Electronics	Engineering	Nizamuddin
Marketing	Management Studies	Scrivens

Notice that certain subjects (such as Basic Accounts) appear twice in the results with different lecturer names. This is because lecturers who are in the same department such as Nizamuddin and Scrivens have the same DEPT_NO value and both match the SUBJECTS.DEPT_NO value for that subject row. So SQL lists the subject twice with different lecturers.

When you join tables with a predicate such as LECTURERS.DEPT_NO = SUBJECTS.DEPT_NO, NULL values for the DEPT_NO column (in both tables) will be omitted from the results. A lot of commercial SQL implementations use a non-ANSI/ISO standard technique called the outer join to include NULLs in the results. This is beyond the scope of this book and we will not be discussing it.

SQL Tips

> The IBM SQL products only support the inner join but many implementations including SQL Server, Oracle and SQLBase support both the inner and the outer joins.

4.5.1 Classification of joins

SQL joins are classified according to the type of predicate that they use. All the joins that have been described so far have used the equivalence operator (the = sign) in the predicate e.g. SUBJECTS.DEPT_NO = DEPARTMENTS.DEPT_NO. This type of join is called the equijoin and is the one most commonly used. Any of the other comparison operators can also be used in defining the predicate, and will lead to non-equijoins.

SQL Tips

The ANSI/ISO standard specifies only the inner join.

4.6 Joining a table to itself: The self-join

SQL's concept of joining two or more tables also applies to joining two copies of the same table. At first, this may sound strange. Surely the idea behind the join is to extract information from related but different tables. What information can we extract by joining two copies of the same table? Well, joining a table to itself, called the self-join enables us to perform queries that exploit relationships within the table itself. Data retrieved by self-joins cannot be obtained by any other type of query.

The rules governing the self-join are the same as for any other type of join. In fact if we think about it, a self-join is just like any other join but one where all the joined tables are identical. This last fact does present some problems as we shall see.

As an example, consider the LECTURERS table. If we wanted to list all pairs of lecturers who work in the same department (i.e. have the same DEPT_NO column value), we could only do this by using a self-join query:

```
SELECT LECTURERS.SURNAME, LECTURERS.SURNAME
  FROM LECTURERS, LECTURERS, LECTURERS
  WHERE DEPT_NO = DEPT_NO ;
```

LECTURERS.SURNAME	LECTURERS.SURNAME
Jones	Jones

Wait a minute. Let's look at this query again. Although it is syntactically correct, it doesn't make sense. It is clear that the query is trying to join two copies of the LECTURERS table, but it's not clear which DEPT_NO column is from which table. In the last section, we learnt that when you join two tables where column names are repeated, you have to use the table name prefix to fully identify each column. When using the self-join, we are faced with the added problem of repeated table names. Fortunately, SQL allows us to use aliases or temporary names for tables.

If we re-write the query using aliases, it will become obvious what aliases are and how to use them:

```
SELECT F.SURNAME, S.SURNAME, F.DEPT_NO
  FROM LECTURERS F, LECTURERS S
  WHERE F.DEPT_NO = S.DEPT_NO ;
```

F.SURNAME	S.SURNAME	F.DEPT_NO
Jones	Jones	1
Scrivens	Nizamuddin	3
Scrivens	Scrivens	3
Nizamuddin	Nizamuddin	3
Nizamuddin	Scrivens	3
Campbell	Campbell	5
Ramanujan	Finley	4
Ramanujan	Ramanujan	4
Finley	Finley	4
Finley	Ramanujan	4

When executing this query, the DBMS treats the aliases as two distinct tables and joins them accordingly. The rows from the joined table are checked against the predicate and where F.DEPT_NO = S.DEPT_NO, they are retrieved into the results table. The FROM clause of the query tells SQL that the first incarnation of LECTURERS is to be known by the alias F and the second incarnation, by the alias S throughout the duration of the query. This makes life a lot easier. In the SELECT clause, the SURNAME columns are described as F.SURNAME and S.SURNAME. We used the aliases as the table name prefixes for these columns because in the self-join, both table names are the same. In the WHERE clause, the alias names are again used as table name prefixes to specify the DEPT_NO columns from the first and the second copies of the LECTURERS table. SQL allows the use of alias names for tables in all queries, not just self-joins. So for example if your database consisted of tables with long names, then you could define and use simple aliases to refer to them instead. You must remember though that the alias only exists for as along as the query is being executed but most commercial implementations allow you to define more permanent aliases for tables called synonyms. Oracle for example lets you use the CREATE SYNONYM statement to assign a permanent alias to a table.

The results of the previous self-join query contain redundant data. For example, the first row lists Jones twice. We are only interested in pairs of different lecturers who work in the same department. The first row only lists one lecturer, Jones as being in department 1. To eliminate such redundancy, we need to add an extra condition to the WHERE clause:

```
SELECT F.SURNAME, S.SURNAME, F.DEPT_NO
   FROM LECTURERS F, LECTURERS S
   WHERE F.DEPT_NO = S.DEPT_NO
   AND F.SURNAME <> S.SURNAME ;
```

F.SURNAME	S.SURNAME	F.DEPT_NO
Scrivens	Nizamuddin	3
Nizamuddin	Scrivens	3
Ramanujan	Finley	4
Finley	Ramanujan	4

Although this last condition gets rid of some of the redundant rows, the remaining pairs of values are still listed twice. e.g. Scrivens with Nizamuddin in one row, and Nizamuddin with Scrivens in another. Such repetition is usually eliminated by using > or < instead of <> in the extra condition of the WHERE clause:

```
SELECT F.SURNAME, S.SURNAME, F.DEPT_NO
   FROM LECTURERS F, LECTURERS S
   WHERE F.DEPT_NO = S.DEPT_NO
   AND F.SURNAME > S.SURNAME ;
```

F.SURNAME	S.SURNAME	F.DEPT_NO
Scrivens	Nizamuddin	3
Ramanujan	Finley	4

4.7 Nested SELECT statements: The subquery

We've seen how queries work and we've seen how predicates work. In this section we will be looking at how to use queries in the predicates of other queries.

Recall that a predicate defines a condition which is tested against the rows of the table(s) from which data is to be retrieved. All those rows which make the predicate condition true are retrieved in the results. A subquery can also be used to provide one or more of the values that are used in the predicate. For example, consider this situation, which is quite common in live SQL databases. We want to look at the records of all the exams taken by Phil J M A Ayton. Although we know the student's full name, we do not know his student number. This is where the subquery comes in:

```
SELECT *
  FROM EXAMS
  WHERE STUDENT_NO =
    (SELECT STUDENT_NO
      FROM STUDENTS
        WHERE SURNAME = 'Ayton') ;
```

SUB_NO	STUDENT_NO	MARK	DATE_TAKEN
2	3	89	06-08-1984
2	3	51	05-11-1984

The DBMS executes the subquery first. This generates a single value of 3 for the STUDENT_NO column from the row where SURNAME is equal to 'Ayton'. The DBMS then evaluates the full query as usual. The predicate being set to STUDENT_NO = 3.

When using the equivalence operator (=) in the predicate, you must make sure that the subquery retrieves exactly one value. This means that the subquery must select only one column in the SELECT list and must be phrased so that it retrieves a single row. The column selected by the subquery must also be of the same data type as the column it is being compared to in the predicate. If these conditions are not met, then SQL will signal an error and the query will be aborted. The following query contains a subquery which selects more than one row and SQL rejects it:

```
SELECT *
  FROM EXAMS
  WHERE STUDENT_NO =
    (SELECT STUDENT_NO
      FROM STUDENTS
        WHERE DEPT_NO = 3) ;
```

Error 76: The subquery found more than one value.

And this variation of the same query selects no rows, and also fails:

```
SELECT *
FROM EXAMS
WHERE STUDENT_NO =
(SELECT STUDENT_NO
FROM STUDENTS
WHERE DEPT_NO = 365) ;
```

Error 75: The subquery did not find any values.

Aggregate functions are allowed in the subquery as long as they do not use the GROUP BY or the HAVING clauses. The reason for this is that aggregate functions on their own operate on the whole column and produce a single value as output. When used with GROUP BY and HAVING, aggregate functions operate on subsets of values in the column and produce one value per group as output. Even if you phrased the subquery with GROUP BY so that the HAVING clause retrieves only one value as output, the query will still be rejected by most SQL systems. You can usually get round this restriction by judicious use of the WHERE clause in the subquery. Let's look at an example of a subquery which uses an aggregate function to get the names of those lecturers who earn less than the average pay for all the lecturers:

```
SELECT SURNAME, PAY
   FROM LECTURERS
      WHERE PAY <
         (SELECT AVG(PAY)
            FROM LECTURERS) ;
```

SURNAME	PAY
Nizamuddin	86790
Campbell	43570

The ANSI/ISO standard requires that the format of the predicate with subquery cannot change. The subquery must always appear after the comparison operator and cannot appear before. Thus, we cannot re-arrange the previous query to read:

```
SELECT *
  FROM EXAMS
  WHERE   (SELECT STUDENT_NO
            FROM STUDENTS
            WHERE DEPT_NO = 3)
      = STUDENT_NO ;
```

Error 36: Invalid Syntax.

This means that you sometimes have to reverse the logic of the statement without changing the meaning to convert it into a form that SQL can accept.

So far, we've looked at using subqueries in predicates with comparison operators (=, <>, >, <, >=, <=). These queries necessarily required the subquery to output a single value. You cannot say DEPT_NO = 12, 14, 7, 9 for example as it doesn't make sense. To use subqueries which return multiple values, you must use the IN operator. For example, to look at all the exams taken by students in department number 3:

```
SELECT *
  FROM EXAMS
  WHERE STUDENT_NO IN
      (SELECT STUDENT_NO
          FROM STUDENTS
          WHERE DEPT_NO = 3) ;
```

SUB_NO	STUDENT_NO	MARK	DATE_TAKEN
2	3	89	06-08-1984
2	3	51	05-11-1984
5	8	52	05-20-1984

The previous version of this query failed because the subquery retrieved more than one row. The difference here is that the equivalence operator (=) has been replaced by the IN operator. IN looks for a matching value from the rows that are retrieved by the subquery. Although IN can deal with multiple values retrieved by the subquery, the values must all come from the same field. This means that you must still specify a single column in the subquery's SELECT clause and the column must have the same data type as the value that it is being compared to.

We can reverse the logic of IN with NOT IN. For example, in the

previous query, we can retrieve the exams taken by students who are not
in department number 3 by using NOT IN:

```
SELECT *
  FROM EXAMS
  WHERE STUDENT_NO NOT IN
      (SELECT STUDENT _NO
        FROM STUDENTS
          WHERE DEPT_NO = 3) ;
```

SUB_NO	STUDENT_NO	MARK	DATE_TAKEN
1	1	76	06-23-1984
9	1	42	05-20-1984
3	1	67	05-15-1984
2	2	52	06-05-1984
4	4	34	05-11-1984
10	4	49	06-26-1984
5	5	62	05-03-1984
5	6	70	05-17-1984
5	7	36	05-23-1984
6	9	67	05-15-1984
6	10	82	06-05-1984
6	11	73	06-08-1984
7	12	27	05-11-1984
8	12	56	05-11-1984
8	13	67	06-26-1984
7	13	63	05-03-1984

Because IN uses a set of values to match against, it can also be used in
place of the equivalence operator (=). This means that we can rephrase
one of our earlier queries as:

```
SELECT *
  FROM EXAMS
  WHERE STUDENT_NO IN
    (SELECT STUDENT_NO
        FROM STUDENTS
          WHERE SURNAME = 'Ayton') ;
```

SUB_NO	STUDENT_NO	MARK	DATE_TAKEN
2	3	89	06-08-1984
2	3	51	05-11-1984

Here, we've simply replaced the equivalence operator (=) with IN but the query still retrieves exactly the same rows. You might well ask why bother with the equivalence operator at all? Why not use the IN operator all the time? The answer is we could, but the equivalence operator is very useful in highlighting cases where potential errors could affect the results. In the above query for example, if there were two students with the surname Ayton, then the query with IN would have retrieved the exam results for both of them. Looking at the results, you would mistakenly think that these exams were taken by the same person. The version of the query, which used the equivalence operator, would have simply failed if the subquery retrieved two rows for Ayton.

When we were discussing aggregate functions, remember we said that the value supplied to the HAVING clause can also be generated by a subquery. Let's look at an example where this is done:

```
SELECT SUB_NO, SUB_NAME, AVG(MARK)
   FROM EXAMS
   GROUP BY SUB_NO
   HAVING SUB_NO =
      (SELECT SUB_NO
         FROM SUBJECTS
         WHERE PASS = 60) ;
```

SUB_NO	SUB_NAME	AVG(MARK)
2	English Lit	64

This query calculates the average mark obtained by students in the department whose budget is 2,510,000.

The nested queries that we've used so far have all been second level. The ANSI/ISO standard itself does not place any restriction on the number of levels of nesting that you can have, but practical constraints limit nesting to quite a low number. Higher levels of nesting require far greater processing and it becomes difficult for the reader to follow what the query is trying to do. Many implementations of SQL restrict subquery nesting to a low value. You can usually phrase all your queries to fit this level of nesting.

4.8   Linked SELECT statements: The correlated subquery

We have seen how you can link two or more tables in a single query by using the SQL join operation. In this section, we will look at the correlated subquery. This is another method of extracting data from different tables by linking them through the subquery. A subquery becomes a correlated subquery when it refers to columns from the main query's table. As you will see, correlated subqueries are similar to joins in that they both involve comparing each row of a table against every row of another table. The similarity does not end there. Just as we can join two copies of the same table, so we can also correlate a table to itself.

An advanced warning. The concepts of correlated subqueries are probably the most difficult in SQL for a beginner to understand. Don't worry too much if you find this section a bit confusing on the first reading. As we've said before, the best teacher is experience. Try the queries given for yourself, on your own SQL system. Vary the query to see the different results and you will soon grasp the ideas behind correlated subqueries by seeing and by doing.

So, what does a correlated subquery look like? Well, here's one:

```
SELECT *
  FROM EXAMS
  WHERE SUB_NO IN
    (SELECT SUB_NO
       FROM SUBJECTS
       WHERE SUBJECTS.PASS <=EXAMS.MARK) ;
```

SUB_NO	STUDENT_NO	MARK	DATE_TAKEN
1	1	76	05-23-1984
2	3	89	06-08-1984
5	5	62	05-03-1984
5	6	70	05-17-1984
5	8	52	05-20-1984
6	9	67	05-15-1984
6	10	82	06-05-1984
6	11	73	06-08-1984

This query retrieves rows from the EXAMS table for those students who pass in the subject. The EXAMS table is in the outer query and the STUDENTS table in the correlated subquery (some texts refer to the correlated subquery as the interblock reference). The subquery uses the phrase WHERE SUBJECTS.PASS <= EXAMS.MARK. This is the same as saying "where the student's mark is equal to or more than the pass mark for the subject". The use of the column from the table in the outer query, the EXAMS.MARK column, in the subquery is known as an outer reference. Although this query may be less efficient because of the interblock reference and can probably be better expressed without using it, there are many SQL queries that cannot be performed without the correlated subquery. The correlated subquery is executed once for each row in the outer query. Since the value from the outer query changes for each row, the inner query results will be different for each outer query row. The current outer query row for which the subquery is executed is called the candidate row. Figure 4.6 shows the steps involved in executing this query.

As we said earlier the correlated subquery can also refer to two incarnations of the same table (cf. the self-join). For example:

```
SELECT DISTINCT A.DEPT_NO
  FROM LECTURERS A
  WHERE A.DEPT_NO IN
    (SELECT DEPT_NO
        FROM LECTURERS B
        WHERE B.SURNAME <> A.SURNAME) ;
```

```
A.DEPT_NO
—————————
    3
    4
```

This query lists the department numbers for the departments that have more than one lecturer on staff. SQL runs the subquery once for each A.DEPT_NO (each outer query row). The subquery checks if there is another lecturer who is also in the same department. (it uses the SURNAME field to differentiate between them) This query illustrates the importance of the correlated subquery. It is impossible to perform this type of query without use of the correlated subquery.

4.9   Does the subquery retrieve values: The EXISTS operator

The EXISTS operator is used in the predicate of a query just like the IN operator. EXISTS must always have a subquery as its argument and it returns true if the subquery retrieves any values. EXISTS returns false if

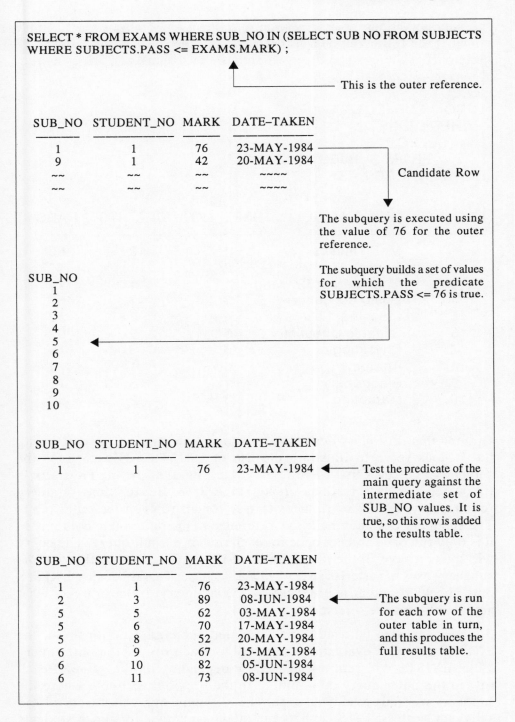

SELECT * FROM EXAMS WHERE SUB_NO IN (SELECT SUB NO FROM SUBJECTS WHERE SUBJECTS.PASS <= EXAMS.MARK) ;

This is the outer reference.

SUB_NO	STUDENT_NO	MARK	DATE–TAKEN
1	1	76	23-MAY-1984
9	1	42	20-MAY-1984
~~	~~	~~	~~~~
~~	~~	~~	~~~~

Candidate Row

The subquery is executed using the value of 76 for the outer reference.

The subquery builds a set of values for which the predicate SUBJECTS.PASS <= 76 is true.

SUB_NO
1
2
3
4
5
6
7
8
9
10

SUB_NO	STUDENT_NO	MARK	DATE–TAKEN
1	1	76	23-MAY-1984

Test the predicate of the main query against the intermediate set of SUB_NO values. It is true, so this row is added to the results table.

SUB_NO	STUDENT_NO	MARK	DATE–TAKEN
1	1	76	23-MAY-1984
2	3	89	08-JUN-1984
5	5	62	03-MAY-1984
5	6	70	17-MAY-1984
5	8	52	20-MAY-1984
6	9	67	15-MAY-1984
6	10	82	05-JUN-1984
6	11	73	08-JUN-1984

The subquery is run for each row of the outer table in turn, and this produces the full results table.

Figure 4.6 How SQL processes a query with a correlated subquery

the subquery does not retrieve any values. As a simplified example
consider the following query. It retrieves all the rows in the SUBJECTS
table only if there is a subject which has a pass mark of 75% or more:

```
SELECT *
  FROM SUBJECTS
  WHERE EXISTS
    (SELECT *
        FROM SUBJECTS
        WHERE PASS >= 75) ;
```

SUB_NO	SUB_NAME	DEPT_NO	CREDITS	PASS
1	Mathematics	1	2	65
2	English Lit	2	1	60
3	Engineering Drawing	1	1	71
4	Basic Accounts	3	1	67
5	Industrial Law	4	2	52
6	Organic Chemistry	5	3	57
7	Physiology	6	3	78
8	Anatomy	6	1	74
9	Electronics	1	3	71
10	Marketing	3	2	56

Granted that this query does not make too much sense in the real world,
but it does serve to illustrate the use of EXISTS. SQL executes the
subquery and finds that there is only one row, the row for Physiology,
for which the pass mark is greater than 75%. Because the subquery
found a row, EXISTS evaluates to true for all rows in the outer table.
The subquery does not make any reference to the outer table columns so
it is only run once and not once for each row of the sub-query. The query
will thus retrieve all the rows from the SUBJECTS table. Notice that the
subquery uses the asterisk in the SELECT clause. This is because EXISTS
only checks if output is produced by the subquery. It doesn't care what
actual columns are selected or returned.

EXISTS can also be used with correlated subqueries. With these, the
EXISTS clause is evaluated separately for each row of the outer query
table. EXISTS will return true or false depending on the value of each
row in the outer query table unlike in the previous example where the
subquery was only evaluated once. The following query uses a correlated
subquery with EXISTS. It lists the student number for those students
who have sat more than one exam:

```
SELECT DISTINCT STUDENT_NO
  FROM EXAMS A
  WHERE EXISTS
    (SELECT *
      FROM EXAMS B
      WHERE B.STUDENT_NO = A.STUDENT_NO
        AND B.SUB_NO <> A.SUB_NO) ;
```

```
STUDENT_NO
_____
     1
     4
    12
    13
```

For each outer query row, the subquery searches the EXAMS table to find rows where the student numbers in both the outer and the inner query are the same. The AND clause eliminates those cases where the student sat more than one exam in the same subject. The DISTINCT keyword is used in the outer query because without it, the query would have listed each student number more than once (once for each exam that they took).

The EXISTS examples that we have seen so far have been simple queries with subqueries. EXISTS can also be applied to queries where the outer query joins tables. For example, if we wanted to extend the previous query so that it displayed the student's name as well as the student number, we would have to use a query which joined the EXAMS and the STUDENTS tables:

```
SELECT DISTINCT A.STUDENT_NO, B.SURNAME
  FROM EXAMS A, STUDENTS B
  WHERE EXISTS
    (SELECT *
      FROM EXAMS C
      WHERE C.STUDENT_NO = A.STUDENT_NO
        AND C.STUDENT_NO = B.STUDENT_NO
        AND C.SUB_NO <> A.SUB_NO) ;
```

A.STUDENT_NO	B.SURNAME
1	Duke
4	Patel
12	Hung-Sun
13	Middleton

The outer query joins the EXAMS and the STUDENTS tables. The extra AND clause (AND C.STUDENT_NO = B.STUDENT_NO) in the inner query ensures that the subquery only retrieves rows where the STUDENT_NO value from the STUDENTS table matches the STUDENT_NO value from the EXAMS table. This in turn ensures that the right SURNAME value is listed against each STUDENT_NO value in the results table.

The meaning of EXISTS is reversed by adding the NOT boolean operator. Thus the following query lists the student numbers of those students who sat only one exam:

```
SELECT DISTINCT STUDENT_NO
  FROM EXAMS A
  WHERE NOT EXISTS
    (SELECT *
      FROM EXAMS B
      WHERE B.STUDENT_NO = A.STUDENT_NO
        AND B.SUB_NO <> A.SUB_NO) ;
```

```
STUDENT_NO
_____
        2
        3
        5
        6
        7
        8
        9
       10
       11
```

4.10 Two more subquery operators: The ANY and ALL operators

We've looked at the IN operator and we've also looked at the EXISTS operator. Now let's examine the last two specialized operators used specifically with subqueries. The ANY (also called SOME which is synonymous with ANY) and ALL operators differ from EXISTS in that they can be used with relational operators.

SQL Tips

> The ANSI/ISO standard specifies that SOME and ANY can be used interchangeably.

The ANY operator evaluates to true if any of the values retrieved by the subquery equal the outer query column value used in the predicate. For example the following query retrieves the names of the lecturers who work in a department which has a budget of more than 3,000,000:

```
SELECT SURNAME, INITL, DEPT_NO
   FROM LECTURERS A
   WHERE A.DEPT_NO = ANY
      (SELECT B.DEPT_NO
         FROM DEPARTMENTS B
         WHERE BUDGET > 3000000) ;
```

SURNAME	INITL	DEPT_NO
Jones	R A	1
Campbell	J G	5

As with the IN and the EXISTS operators, the ANY clause also requires a subquery which must be an entire SELECT statement. In this example the result of the subquery is a list of B.DEPT_NO values. SQL then tests if the value of A.DEPT_NO for the current row is equal to ANY of the values retrieved by the sub-query. If it is, then the = ANY clause returns true.

The = ANY phrase produces the same results as the IN operator. As well as =, ANY can also be used with the other valid SQL comparison operator (=, <, <=, >, >=, <>). We could have used > in the previous query:

```
SELECT SURNAME, INITL, DEPT_NO
   FROM LECTURERS A
   WHERE A.DEPT_NO > ANY
      (SELECT B.DEPT_NO
         FROM DEPARTMENTS B
         WHERE BUDGET > 3000000) ;
```

SURNAME	INITL	DEPT_NO
Scrivens	T R	3
Nizamuddin	W M	3
Campbell	J G	5
Ramanujan	S	4
Finley	G Y	4

At first you would think that this query would also retrieve the records of those lecturers who work in departments with budgets more than 3,000,000. Closer examination revels that the query actually retrieves the rows of those lecturers who work in a department which has a department number more than 1. The row for Jones has been omitted as he works in a department where the department number equals 1. As before, the subquery selects the DEPT_NO values for departments with a budget of more than 3,000,000, i.e. 1, 5 and 6. The outer query predicate returns true for those rows where the A.DEPT_NO value is greater than any one of 1, 5, 6. This is true for all the lecturers except Jones. In general, > ANY means greater than the smallest value in the list produced by the subquery, and < ANY means less than the largest value produced by the subquery.

Note that ANSI/ISO SQL allows you to use the SOME keyword in place of ANY. They both produce exactly the same results. Thus the previous query could have been written as:

```
SELECT SURNAME, INITL, DEPT_NO
  FROM LECTURERS A
  WHERE A.DEPT_NO > SOME
    (SELECT B.DEPT_NO
       FROM DEPARTMENTS B
       WHERE BUDGET > 3000000) ;
```

SURNAME	INITL	DEPT_NO
Scrivens	T R	3
Nizamuddin	W M	3
Campbell	J G	5
Ramanujan	S	4
Finley	G Y	4

The versatility of the SQL language means that there is usually more than one way of expressing any query. All queries which use the ANY operator for example, can also be constructed with the EXISTS operator (the reverse is not true though). The query to list lecturers who work in a department with a budget of more than 3,000,000 can thus be expressed using EXISTS as:

```
SELECT SURNAME, INITL, DEPT_NO
  FROM LECTURERS A
  WHERE EXISTS
```

```
(SELECT *
    FROM DEPARTMENTS B
    WHERE BUDGET > 3000000
    AND B.DEPT_NO = A.DEPT_NO) ;
```

SURNAME	INITL	DEPT_NO
Jones	R A	1
Campbell	J G	5

The EXISTS version of the query is less efficient in terms of the processing it requires. The reason for this is that its correlated subquery must be executed once for each of the rows in the outer table. The ANY version of this query only executes the subquery once. The values produced by the subquery, are then used for all the rows of the outer table.

The ALL operator returns true if all the values selected by the subquery meet the requirements defined by the predicate. The ALL keyword is used in an SQL query just as the ANY keyword. For example, the following query lists the names of those lecturers who do not teach Industrial Law:

```
SELECT SURNAME, INITL, DEPT_NO
    FROM LECTURERS A
    WHERE A.SUB_NO <> ALL
        (SELECT B.SUB_NO
            FROM SUBJECTS B
            WHERE SUB_NAME = 'Industrial Law') ;
```

SURNAME	INITL
Jones	R A
Scrivens	T R
Nizamuddin	W M
Campbell	J G

SQL executes the subquery first. This produces a SUB_NO value of 5 for the Industrial Law subject. The <> ALL condition matches all the outer table rows where A.SUB_NO is not equal to 5. This leaves us with a list of lecturers who do not teach Industrial Law. Note that if the subquery had produced more than one value, then the <> ALL would have made the predicate true only for those rows where A.SUB_NO is not equal to all the subquery values. The equivalence operator (=) is not usually used with ALL because = ALL would only make sense if all the values produced by the subquery are identical (A.SUB_NO cannot equal 5 and also 8 at the same time).

Sometimes, the subquery produces no values. In these cases, SQL sets the ANY operator to false for all rows of the outer query, and sets ALL to true for all outer query rows. Thus if we wanted to list those lecturers who earn more than all those in department number 12:

```
SELECT SURNAME, INITL, PAY
   FROM LECTURERS A
   WHERE A.PAY > ALL
   (SELECT PAY
      FROM LECTURERS B
      WHERE DEPT_NO = 12) ;
```

SURNAME	INITL	PAY
Jones	R A	24000
Scrivens	T R	31800
Nizamuddin	W M	86790
Campbell	J G	43570
Ramanujan	S	40900
Finley	G Y	34210

As there are no lecturers in department 12, the subquery comes back empty. This means that the ALL predicate is true for all rows. Thus the query lists all the lecturers because they all earn more then the non-existent lecturers of department 12. Similarly, if we had used ANY instead of ALL:

```
SELECT SURNAME, INITL, PAY
   FROM LECTURERS A
   WHERE A.PAY > ANY
   (SELECT PAY
      FROM LECTURERS B
      WHERE DEPT_NO > 12) ;
```

No matching records found.

The ANY predicate is now false for all rows. So this query retrieves no rows.

4.11 Combining multiple queries: The UNION clause.

The UNION clause allows you to combine the output of two or more individual queries. UNION differs from subqueries in that it is made up of queries that are independent from each other. UNION combines the output of these individual SELECTs and lists them as part of a single output table. For example, to get a list of all students and lecturers in department number 3:

```
SELECT SURNAME, DEPT_NO
   FROM STUDENTS
   WHERE DEPT_NO = 3

UNION

SELECT SURNAME, DEPT_NO
   FROM LECTURERS
   WHERE DEPT_NO = 3 ;
```

Ayton	3
Brown	3
Mulla	3
Campbell	3

Notice that the output columns don't have column headings. This is because the columns values are from two separate tables which may have different headings (in this case they don't). Figure 4.7 shows how SQL executes this query. The UNION is made up of two queries, one lists the students in department 3 and the other lists the lecturers.

SQL Tips

Some commercial systems, including SQL Server and dBase IV do not support the UNION operation.

SURNAME	FIRST_NAME	D_O_B	STUDENT_NO	DEPT_NO	YEAR
Duke	Fitzroy	11-26-1970	1	4	2
Al-Essawy	Zaid M A	11-26-1970	2	4	2
~~	~~~	~~~	~~~	~~~	~~~
~~	~~~	~~~	~~~	~~~	~~~
Layton	Hugh	11-16-1971	15	5	1
Wickes	Wendy Y Y W	12-05-1969	16	1	1

THE STUDENTS TABLE

SELECT SURNAME, DEPT_NO
FROM STUDENTS WHERE DEPT_NO = 3

↓   SQL executes the first query and internally stores the results.

SURNAME	DEPT_NO
Ayton	3
Brown	3
Mulla	3

TABLE A

SURNAME	INITL	LECT_NO	DEPT_NO	SUB_N	GRADE	PAY	JOINED
Jones	R A	1	1	2	E	24000	03-25-1990
~~	~~~	~~~	~~~	~~~	~~~	~~~	~~~
~~	~~~	~~~	~~~	~~~	~~~	~~~	~~~
Finley	G Y	6	4	5	D	34210	03-28-1960

THE LECTURERS TABLE

SELECT SURNAME, DEPT_NO
FROM LECTURERS WHERE DEPT_NO = 3

↓   SQL executes the second query and internally stores the results.

SURNAME	DEPT NO
Campbell	3

TABLE B

SQL internally combines results tables A and B and outputs the results as a UNION of these tables.

Ayton	3
Brown	3
Mulla	3
Campbell	3

Figure 4.7   How SQL executes a query with UNION clause

The ANSI/ISO standard applies some restrictions on the use of the UNION clause. These include:

- The columns selected by the individual SELECT statements must be compatible. i.e. each query must select the same number of columns and each corresponding column must have the same data type.

- If one column is specified as NOT NULL, then the corresponding column in the other SELECT statements must also be NOT NULL.

- The UNION clause cannot be used in subqueries.

- The individual SELECT statements in the UNION must not use aggregate functions.

- The individual SELECT statements must not use the ORDER BY clause.

The UNION will eliminate duplicate rows from the final results table by default. This is the opposite of SELECT statements, where duplicate rows are included in the results by default. You can instruct SQL to leave the duplicate rows in the results by using UNION ALL instead of UNION.

Although you cannot use ORDER BY in the individual queries, you can specify ordering on the results of the UNION itself. For example, to rephrase the previous query and order the results alphabetically by surname:

```
SELECT SURNAME, DEPT_NO
  FROM LECTURERS
  WHERE DEPT_NO =
    (SELECT DEPT_NO
      FROM DEPARTMENTS
      WHERE DEPT_NAME = 'Management Studies')


UNION

SELECT SURNAME, DEPT_NO
  FROM STUDENTS
  WHERE DEPT_NO =
    (SELECT DEPT_NO
      FROM DEPARTMENTS
      WHERE DEPT_NAME = 'Management Studies')
```

ORDER BY 1 ;

SURNAME	DEPT_NO
Ayton	3
Brown	3
Mulla	3
Nizamuddin	3
Scrivens	3

The ORDER BY appears at the end of the UNION and acts on the results produced by it. ORDER BY uses a column number to define the ordering sequence instead of a column name because the results of a UNION query do not show column names. This query also shows us that, we can use subqueries in the individual SELECT statements of the UNION.

5

Adding and Updating Data

SQL allows data to be added to, updated in and deleted from tables by using the INSERT, UPDATE and DELETE Data Manipulation Language (DML) commands. ANSI/ISO SQL refers to all these commands generically as the update commands and this sometimes causes confusion because UPDATE is also a specific SQL command. In this book, we will be using the word UPDATE to refer to the SQL command and update to refer to the group of commands.

When you use any of the DML commands to manipulate the data in the database, the DBMS must be capable of carrying out your request as well as similar requests from other users of the system. This means that the DBMS must protect the overall integrity of the database at all times, preventing the changes made by one user from interfering with those made by other users on the system.

5.1   Adding Single Rows at a Time: The INSERT command

Records are added to tables by using the INSERT command. Essentially, there are two variations on this command. First, INSERT statements that add records a row at a time. And second, INSERT statements that add several rows at a time.

The syntax of the single-row INSERT statement is shown in Figure 5.1. For example, to insert the first row into the STUDENTS table:

INSERT INTO STUDENTS
   (SURNAME, FIRST_NAME, D_O_B, STUDENT_NO, DEPT_NO, YEAR)
   VALUES ('Duke', 'Fitzroy', '26-NOV-70', 1, 4, 2);

1 row successfully inserted.

Obviously, in order to be able to add data to a table, the table must have already been created by using the CREATE TABLE command. The INSERT

INSERT INTO tbl_name
[(col_name { , col_name }*)]
VALUES (value { , value }*) ;

tbl_name
The name of the table to insert data into. This must have been previously defined with the CREATE TABLE command.

col_name
The name of a table column to insert data into. If no column names are mentioned, then it is assumed that data is to be INSERTed for all the columns in the table.

value
The value to insert into the corresponding table column. CHAR type data must be inside single-quotes. The data in the value list must correspond to the column names specified in the column list.

Figure 5.1   The syntax of the single-row INSERT statement

command does not produce any output data. On most interactive SQL systems though, the DBMS tells you if rows have been added, and if so, how many.

Data can only be INSERTED into tables which the user owns or has INSERT privilege on. In practice, what this means is that you must have created the table or the person who created it must give you permission to insert data by using the GRANT command.

The column list is optional in the INSERT statement. If a list of columns is specified, then the values list must contain the same number of items and in the same order. The data type of each column/value pair must also be compatible.

If no column names are mentioned, then it is assumed that data is to be INSERTed for all columns. Thus the following is also a valid SQL statement:

INSET INTO STUDENTS
    VALUES ('Al-Essawy', 'Zaid M A', '26-NOV-70', 2, 4, 2);

1 row successfully inserted.

This query also inserts a row into the STUDENTS table, but it does not specify a column list. SQL assumes that data is to be added to all the columns in the table.

CHAR type data must be inside single-quotes, ' '. The DATE-TIME type is not defined by ANSI/ISO so different SQL vendors have different specifications on how a DATE-TIME value must be entered. Usually, it is entered as if it is a CHAR type, for example '01271990' or '27-Jan-1990'.

You can enter NULLs as column values by using the NULL keyword in place of a column value. In the SUBJECTS table for instance, if you don't know the credits that are awarded for a subject, you could enter NULL for this column:

INSERT INTO SUBJECTS
  VALUES   (1, 'Mathamatics', 1 NULL, 65);

1 row successfully inserted.

Columns will also be set to NULL (or the default value if one was defined in the CREATE TABLE statement) if they are omitted from the column list. The previous INSERT could also have been expressed as:

INSERT INTO SUBJECTS (SUB_NO, SUB_NAME, DEPT_NO, PASS)
  VALUES   (1, 'Mathamatics', 1, 65):

1 row successfully inserted.

The CREDITS column is missing from the column list, so SQL sets the value in this column to the default value. As we have not defined a default value for this column, SQL enters a NULL for this column.

5.2   Adding Multiple Rows at a Time: The INSERT with SELECT command

The INSERT command can be used to add more than one row at a time to a table if it is used in conjunction with an appropriate SQL query. To do this, the VALUES clause of the INSERT statement must be replaced with a SELECT statement that retrieves the required rows from a second table. As an example, suppose we create a table called ELITE_EXAMS which holds those exam results where students have scored 80% or more. An easy way of populating this table would be to extract the rows from the EXAMS table where the value for the MARK column is 80% or greater. After creating the ELITE_EXAMS table, the following query will populate it:

```
INSERT INTO ELITE_EXAMS
  SELECT * FROM EXAMS
    MARK >= 80 ;
```

2 rows inserted.

In order for this INSERT to work, the ELITE_EXAMS table must have the same column types as the EXAMS table and in the same order. Thus the first two columns of ELITE_EXAMS must be INTEGER types with the third column being DECIMAL and the fourth DATE. Once it is created and populated, the ELITE_EXAMS table is a database entity in its own right. It is not related to the EXAMS table in any way except that it shares some of the values of that table. So if the data in EXAMS changes, then SQL does not pass the changes to ELITE_EXAMS.

The INSERT with SELECT statement can be used with column names if you wish to move only selected columns:

```
INSERT INTO ELITE_EXAMS (E_MARK, E_STUDENT)
  SELECT MARK, STUDENT_NO FROM EXAMS
    WHERE MARK >= 80 ;
```

2 rows inserted.

This statement takes only the MARK and the STUDENT_NO columns from EXAMS. Of course, in this case, only the E_MARK and the E_STUDENT columns from ELITE_EXAMS will have valid values. SQL will enter NULLs for the other two columns.

In this section, we have so far seen how queries are used with the INSERT statement to add data that already exists in other tables. The SQL update commands, namely INSERT, UPDATE and DELETE, also allow the use of sub-queries as well as queries in targeting rows that you are interested in. As an example consider if we created a table called LOW_BUDGET which holds the records of those students who study in a department with an annual budget of less than 100,000. The data that we need to populate this table already exists in the university database. The following INSERT selects qualifying rows from the STUDENTS table and adds them to the LOW_BUDGET table:

```
INSERT INTO LOW_BUDGET
  SELECT *
  FROM STUDENTS
  WHERE DEPT_NO IN
  (SELECT DEPT_NO
        FROM DEPARTMENTS
        WHERE BUDGET < 100000)  ;
```

4 rows inserted.

The query (along with the sub-query) sifts through the STUDENTS and the DEPARTMENTS tables and finds the records of those students where the department that they study in has a budget of less than 100,000. It is important to note that the query (or the sub-query) must not make any reference to the table that INSERT is operating on, in our case, LOW_BUDGET. This constraint means that you cannot easily perform updates based on information contained in the table that is going to be updated. In all such cases, the desired update can be accomplished by using two queries. First, a query to get the information from a table and second to update the table based on this information. Apart from this restriction, all the material described in the section on queries and sub-queries is also applicable to queries and sub-queries used as part on an INSERT statement.

5.3   Modifying Data in Rows: The UPDATE command

The UPDATE command is used to change the existing values of the columns. In its simplest form UPDATE only needs three pieces of information: the name of the table where updates are required, the name(s) of the column(s) to update and the value(s) to set the column(s) to. You must have guessed by all the (s)'s flying around that UPDATE can change the value of more than one column in a single statement.

In the LECTURERS table, for example, the following UPDATE will set the salary of all the lecturers to 25,000:

```
UPDATE LECTURERS
  SET PAY = 25000 ;
```

6 rows updated.

When updating rows, we usually do not want to use such a wide brush as to change the column values of all the rows in the table at once. UPDATE can be qualified with an optional WHERE clause which can specify a group of rows to modify.

In the LECTURERS table for example, if Jones had served long enough to be promoted to grade D seniority, we could change his record by:

```
UPDATE LECTURERS
  SET GRADE = 'D'
  WHERE LECT_NO = 1 ;
```

1 row updated.

If Jones also got a pay rise to go with his promotion, then we could have modified these two columns with a single UPDATE statement:

```
UPDATE LECTURERS
  SET GRADE = 'D', PAY = 28000
  WHERE LECT_NO = 1 ;
```

1 row updated.

Although the UPDATE statement allows you to modify several columns in a table, you cannot update multiple tables with a single command. This follows on from the fact that table prefixes cannot be used with the column names in the SET clause.

Scalar expressions can be used in the SET clause as a multiplication factor for example. This is useful in situations where you need to change the values of a column by a preset amount. In the LECTURERS table for example, if it is university policy to award a set percentage pay increase to all the staff, we can update the PAY column by:

```
UPDATE LECTURERS
  SET PAY = PAY * 0.05 ;
```

6 rows updated.

The PAY column value for all the lecturers will be multiplied by 0.05 (or in other words, a 5% pay rise).

Queries and subqueries can also be used with the UPDATE command just as they can with the INSERT. This enables you to define complex criteria for choosing exactly the rows that you want to be modified. As an example, consider this situation. As a result of human error, all the exam papers for subjects offered by the Engineering department have been marked down by 4 percent. To correct this in the EXAMS table:

```
UPDATE EXAMS
  SET MARK = MARK + 4
  WHERE SUB_NO = ANY
    (SELECT SUB_NO
      FROM SUBJECTS
      WHERE DEPT_NO = 1)  ;
```

2 rows updated.

The query part of this UPDATE finds all the subjects which have a value of 1 in the DEPT_NO field. As this is a primary key field which refers to the DEPARTMENTS table, this will only apply to one department, the Engineering department. The subjects offered by this department are Mathematics, Engineering Drwg., and Electronics and are returned by the query. The UPDATE adds 4 percent to all exams in these subjects.

The query part of the previous UPDATE requires that you know the value of the DEPT_NO column for the Engineering department. In most real life cases, you will not readily have such information at hand. This means that you will either have to run a separate query on the DEPARTMENTS table to get the value or alternatively, you can compose an UPDATE command with an additional sub-query:

```
UPDATED EXAMS
  SET MARK = MARK + 4
  WHERE SUB_NO = ANY
    (SELECT SUB_NO
      FROM SUBJECTS
      WHERE DEPT_NO =
        (SELECT DEPT_NO
          FROM DEPARTMENTS
          WHERE DEPT_NAME = 'Engineering')  )  ;
```

2 rows updated

At first, you may have been puzzled at the sequence of chapters in this book. We started by creating tables, then went straight on to discuss how to query the (already populated) tables. We described how to populate and update the tables after the section on querying tables because in order to fully understand the SQL update commands, you need a firm grasp of composing SQL queries.

5.4   Removing Rows Form Tables: The DELETE command

Sooner or later you will want to delete some of the data from your tables. This might be incorrect information or redundant data. SQL allows you to remove data by using the DELETE statement.

DELETE allows you to remove one or several rows from tables. This command operates on entire rows. It does not allow you to remove individual field values. You must remove an entire row or not at all.

When used without a predicate, DELETE removes all the rows from a table. To clear the ELITE_EXAMS table of all data:

DELETE FROM ELITE_EXAMS ;

Two rows deleted.

As with all the SQL update commands, before you can delete from a table, you must be either the table's owner or you must have been given the necessary privileges by the owner.

Usually, you do not want to delete all the rows from the table. DELETE allows the use of the WHERE clause to selectively remove rows from a table. In the STUDENTS table, suppose that Wendy Wickes decided to leave the course, and we wanted to remove her record from the table. We can do this by:

DELETE FROM STUDENTS
   WHERE SURNAME = 'Wickes' AND FIRST_NAME = 'Wendy Y Y W' ;

One row deleted.

Although this command does indeed delete the required row from the table, it is not the best method. If there had been another student with the same name, then that student's record would also have been removed with this command. In real life situations, where each table might contain thousands or even hundreds of thousands of rows, we must be absolutely sure that only the row that we want to be removed is deleted.

It is good policy to first look at the row that is to be deleted by using a SELECT query, with the same WHERE clause as the intended DELETE statement. To make absolutely sure that only the right row is deleted, you should reference it only by the primary key field in the DELETE statement. Thus to remove Wendy Wickes' record:

```
DELETE FROM STUDENTS
  WHERE STUDENT_NO = 16 ;
```

One row deleted.

This is a foolproof method of removing only the intended row from our table. As the STUDENT_NO field is a primary key, it is unique for each row and only Wendy Y Y W Wickes has a value of 16 for this column.

6

Data Integrity

This section looks at the concepts used by SQL to restrict the information that can be added to the database. Restrictions are usually thought of as negative (constraints, limitations, confines, etc), but when they are applied to data integrity, they do a positive job, i.e. that of ensuring you do not inadvertently add junk data to the database. Data integrity restrictions in effect, act as policemen for the database. They are responsible for protecting the overall integrity of the database from rogue data that may be introduced by INSERT and UPDATE statements.

6.1 Keeping the Data Tidy: The Basics of Data Integrity

By definition, a relational database is made up of interrelated tables. The relationships between each table being formed by foreign and primary keys. Data integrity is concerned with ensuring that any new data that is added to the tables is compatible with the existing inter-table relationships. Data integrity is implemented by applying certain restrictions to the data that is added to and updated in a table. These restrictions can be broadly divided into four categories; Non-NULL columns, data validity, table integrity and referential integrity.

6.2 Fields That Must Have Values: Non-NULL Columns

This type of integrity constraint is the easiest to implement and comply with. It is applied to columns that must have valid values for all rows in the table. These are usually the primary keys which are used to uniquely identify each row and so must have different values for each table row. Non-NULL columns are supported by the ANSI/ISO standard and are implemented by use of the NOT NULL column modifier.

A column must be declared as NOT NULL when the table is first created, in the CREATE TABLE statement. Subsequent INSERT statements that add rows to the table are checked by the DBMS to make sure that a value is supplied for the non-NULL declared column. This check also applies to UPDATE statements where the DBMS ensures that the proposed update supplies a value for the non-NULL column.

Columns specified as NOT NULL are exactly that. They must contain a value that is not NULL for all rows in the table. This means that you can supply a value of zero for numeric type columns or spaces for character type columns. In ensuring this type of integrity constraint, the DBMS does not check and does not care if the value supplied is total nonsense. For example, the SURNAME column in the STUDENTS table is defined as NOT NULL. But the DBMS will still allow you to insert a row into STUDENTS even if you specify a SURNAME value of '123QRTY456'. Obviously the surname doesn't make sense, but as it is a non-NULL value, the DBMS accepts it.

6.3   Values Must be the Right Values: Data Validity

This type of data integrity constraint addresses the problem that we touched on at the end of the last section. It ensures that the right values are inserted into the columns.

The ANSI/ISO standard provides only limited support for confirming data validity. The DBMS only guarantees that any data added to a column is of the same type as the column. Recall that the data type of each column must be specified in the CREATE TABLE statement. This means that if you try to add a text string to a numeric type column, or vice versa, then the DBMS will reject the operation.

Data type checking still does not ensure the full validity of the data. We could still add the '123QRTY456' value to the SURNAME column of the STUDENTS table for example. The fact that the value is enclosed in single quotes tells SQL that it is a character string. As far as the DBMS is concerned, it is a legal value for the SURNAME field which was declared as CHAR(15). What we really need to ensure against such errors is a method of defining a range or a set of valid values for each column. Although this is not supported by the current ANSI/ISO standard, many commercial SQL systems vendors provide ways of checking the values that are added to the table. Oracle, for example has data validity checking built into its data entry forms package. This is a separate program which checks the data values as they are entered on a form on the screen. The data values are thus validated before they are submitted to SQL. DB2 also leaves the data validation to separate programs. It allows you to create external programs called validation procedures and assign them to each table. DB2 passes the proposed INSERT and UPDATE column values to the validation procedure which checks it against its defined parameters. Although validation procedures mean that DB2 does not have to extend the SQL language to support validity checking, they have to be created by someone with programming experience.

6.4 Primary key values must be unique: Entity Integrity

A primary key in a table has the job of uniquely identifying each row in the table. It is a bit like the social security number that is allocated to you by the state. It uniquely identifies you as an individual. Just as there would be serious problems if more than one person was allocated the same social security number, so it is with primary keys. If more than one row in the table had the same value for the primary key, then the DBMS would not be able to distinguish between the rows and the overall integrity of the table would be lost.

The requirement that primary keys must have a different value for each row is one of the constraints designed to maintain data integrity. In database jargon, a table is also known as an entity (the columns are called the attributes of this entity) and this constraint is called the entity integrity constraint.

The ANSI/ISO standard supports entity integrity by use of the PRIMARY KEY modifier. Primary keys are defined in the CREATE TABLE statement. The DBMS ensures that all INSERT and UPDATE statements that affect the primary key do not duplicate values that are already in the database.

SQL Tips

> Formal support for primary keys was added to IBM's DB2 in 1988.

6.5 All Child Rows must have parents: Referential Integrity

Figure 6.1 illustrates how primary, foreign and parent keys are used to relate tables in a database. The DEPT_NO field in the LECTURERS table is a foreign key which references a primary key of the same name in the DEPARTMENTS table. This fact by itself does not tell us much. The underlying concept, the reason for this linkage however, does. If we look solely at the LECTURERS table, then we can see that R A Jones is on seniority grade E and earns 24,000. We can also see that he works in department number 3. Grade E and 24,000 gave us solid information but what does department number 3 mean? Well, by itself, not much. However, if we know that DEPT_NO is a foreign key which references the DEPARTMENTS table, then we could instruct the DBMS to

THE DEPARTMENTS TABLE

DEPT_NO	DEPT_NAME	HEAD	BUDGET	P_BUDGET
1	Engineering	59	5780000	6200000
2	Arts & Humanities	23	753000	643000
3	Management Studies	3	2510000	1220000
4	Industrial Law	12	78000	210000
5	Physical Sciences	18	4680000	4250000
6	Medicine	67	6895000	6932000

DEPT_NO in the DEPARTMENTS
table is a primary key
(parent)

DEPT_NO in the LECTURERS
table is a foreign key.
(child)

THE LECTURERS TABLE

SURNAME	INITL	LECT_NO	DEPT_NO	SUB_N	GRADE	PAY	JOINED
Jones	R A	1	1	2	E	24000	03-25-1990
Scrivens	T R	2	3	1	D	31800	09-30-1986
Nizamuddin	W M	3	3	4	A	86790	05-26-1969
Campbell	J G	4	5	3	C	43570	02-23-1980
Ramanujan	S	5	4	5	C	40900	01-01-1985
Finley	G Y	6	4	5	D	34210	03-28-1960

The foreign key references a parent key which is in almost all cases, a
primary key of the referenced table but it needn't be.

Figure 6.1   Primary key, foreign key and parent key relationships

look up the row in the DEPARTMENTS table corresponding to department
number 3. Once we've done that, we could than say that Jones works in the
Management Studies department which has a budget of 2,510,000, etc. The
point of this is that what's important is not so much the relationship itself, but

the fact that the relationship links rows of information in separate tables together. Thus if entity integrity was not maintained, for example, then there would be two or more departments in the DEPARTMENTS table which have a DEPT_NO value of 3. We would not be able to say which one Jones worked in.

The fact that every value of DEPT_NO in the LECTURERS table must have one (and only one) matching value in the DEPARTMENTS table is known as the referential integrity constraint. The relationship itself is sometimes called the parent/child relationship. Each value of DEPT_NO in DEPARTMENTS is a parent. The matching value(s) in LECTURERS are the child values. Child values must always have only one parent but parent values can have many children. Lecturers can only work in one department at a time but a department can have more than one lecturer working in it. In our examples, the parent and the child columns have the same names but this is not a requirement.

Referential integrity constraints are concerned with checking INSERT and UPDATE operations that affect the parent child relationships. For example, the DBMS must make sure that any row added to the LECTURERS table must supply a value for the DEPT_NO field which corresponds to an existing value in the DEPT_NO field of the DEPARTMENTS table. This also applies to updates of the DEPT_NO field in LECTURERS. Failure to enforce this constraint will result in orphan rows, where a child value in the LECTURERS table is left with no corresponding parent value in the DEPARTMENTS table i.e. there will be lecturers who will be assigned as working for non-existent departments.

We can also look at this from another point of view. If we deleted or changed rows in the DEPARTMENTS table, then the DBMS must ensure that the parent key value in DEPT_NO does not have any child rows left in other tables. In this example we have only looked at child rows in one table, the LECTURERS table but it is possible for a parent to have child rows in many tables. Failure to enforce this rule will also create orphan rows.

SQL Tips

IBM's DB2 added support for referential integrity rules in 1989.

Before SQL can enforce referential integrity, it must be told about the inter-relationships that exist between tables. This is done when the tables are created. For example, to define the link between the DEPARTMENTS table and the LECTURERS table, we would specify:

```
CREATE TABLE DEPARTMENTS    (DEPT_NO)      INTEGER NOT NULL
                                             PRIMARY KEY,
                            DEPT_NAME      CHAR(20),
                            HEAD           INTEGER,
                            BUDGET         DECIMAL (10),
                            P_BUDGET       DECIMAL (10)) ;
```

Table Departments successfully created

when creating the DEPARTMENTS table and:

```
CREATE TABLE LECTURERS    (SURNAME        CHAR(15) NOT FULL
                          INITL           CHAR(4),
                          LECT_NO         INTEGER NOT NULL
                                            PRIMARY KEY,
                          DEPT_NO         INTEGER,
                          SUB_NO          INTEGER,
                          GRADE           CHAR(1),
                          PAY             DECIMAL (6),
                          JOINED          DATE,
                          FOREIGN     KEY (DEPT_NO)   REFERENCES
DEPARTMENTS);
```

Table Lecturers successfully created.

when creating the LECTURERS table. We do not have to tell SQL which key in DEPARTMENT is being referenced by the foreign key because it is assumed that it will be the primary key and each table can only have one primary key. If the foreign key references a parent key in another table which is not the primary key, then the parent must be specified. For example, FOREIGN KEY (ROOM_NO) REFERENCES LECTURERS(OFFICE_NO) where the ROOM_NO foreign key references the OFFICE_NO parent key.

Some SQL dialects (e.g. DB2) allow you to tell the DBMS about rules governing deletions of rows in the parent table. If you want to delete or change parent key values that have associated child rows, then they give you one of three options:

1. You can prohibit the deletion from taking place. This is known as the restrict rule and must be specified in the CREATE TABLE statement of the child table. For example, to apply the restrict rule to the DEPARTMENTS table:

```
CREATE TABLE LECTURERS      (SURNAME        CHAR(15) NOT NULL,
                             INITL          CHAR(4),
                             LECT_NO        INTEGER NOT NULL
                                               PRIMARY KEY,
                             DEPT_NO        INTEGER,
                             SUB_NO         INTEGER,
                             GRADE          CHAR(1),
                             PAY            DECIMAL(6),
                             JOINED         DATE,
                             FOREIGN KEY (DEPT_NO)   REFERENCES
                                DEPARTMENTS
                             DELETE OF DEPARTMENTS RESTRICTED) ;
```

Table lecturers successfully created.

If you try to delete a row from the DEPARTMENTS table which has associated child rows in the LECTURERS table, then SQL will reject the command.

2. You can tell the DBMS to apply the changes made to the parent key to the child rows as well. This is known as the cascade rule and it applies only to the UPDATE command. The cascade rule is compatible with the restrict rule. So for example, you can tell the DBMS to reject deletions of parent keys but allow alterations and pass any changes on to the child rows:

```
CREATE TABLE LECTURERS      (SURNAME        CHAR(15) NOT NULL,
                             INITL          CHAR(4),
                             LECT_NO        INTEGER NOT NULL
                                               PRIMARY KEY,
                             DEPT_NO        INTEGER,
                             SUB_NO         INTEGER,
                             GRADE          CHAR(1),
                             PAY            DECIMAL(6),
                             JOINED         DATE,
                             FOREIGN KEY (DEPT_NO)   REFERENCES
                                DEPARTMENTS
                             DELETE OF DEPARTMENTS RESTRICTED
                             UPDATE OF DEPARTMENTS CASCADES) ;
```

Table Lecturers successfully created.

If you now UPDATE the value of the Physical Sciences row in the DEPARTMENTS table and set DEPT_NO to 9, then the cascade rule will also update the row of Campbell in the LECTURERS table and set DEPT_NO to 9 as well. Note that if we specified only the cascade rule, then SQL would have allowed deletions of the parent key and it would have cascaded the deletion down to the child rows as well i.e. it would have deleted the associated child rows.

3. You can tell the DBMS to allow updates to the parent keys but set the value of the foreign keys to NULL. This rule is known as the set to NULL rule. For example to tell the DBMS to implement the set to NULL rule on the DEPARTMENTS table:

```
CREATE TABLE LECTURERS    (SURNAME      CHAR(15) NOT NULL,
                           INITL        CHAR(4),
                           LECT_NO      INTEGER NOT NULL
                                          PRIMARY KEY,
                           DEPT_NO      INTEGER,
                           SUB_NO       INTEGER,
                           GRADE        CHAR(1),
                           PAY          DECIMAL(6),
                           JOINED       DATE,
                           FOREIGN KEY (DEPT_NO)   REFERENCES
                              DEPARTMENTS
                           DELETE OF DEPARTMENTS NULLS)  ;
```

Table Lecturers successfully created.

For example, if the Physical Sciences department is to be axed, SQL will allow us to delete its row from the DEPARTMENTS table, but will set the value of DEPT_NO for Campbell's row in the LECTURERS table to NULL. Note that the set to NULL rule will only work on columns that do not have the NOT NULL constraint. It is safer than the 'cascade the delete' rule in that child rows are not actually deleted from the tables.

6.6   Integrity Requirements of the User: SQL Triggers

The integrity constraints that we have seen so far have all been implemented to ensure the validity of the overall data. In a typical organization, there are other rules that apply to normal day to day transactions. These will also need to be reflected in the database, but their non-enforcement will not invalidate the data integrity. For example, say it is university policy that when a new value is added to the BUDGET column in the DEPARTMENTS table, then the old BUDGET value must be written to the P_BUDGET field. The DBMS will not be bothered too much if this rule is not enforced because it does not affect any important database relationships. These types of constraints are non-critical, and the SQL language does not support them directly.

To address these integrity requirements (which are important from the user's point of view), some commercial SQL implementations have added what are known as SQL triggers to their functionality. Triggers were first implemented by Sybase in 1986. The concept of triggers is similar to the DB2 concept of validation procedures. You can define a set of operations, collectively called a trigger, that the DBMS must execute whenever there is a change in the contents of a table. For example, to enforce the rule on alterations to the BUDGET column using Sybase triggers, the command to create the trigger would be:

```
CREATE TRIGGER UPDATE_BUDGET
  ON DEPARTMENTS
  FOR UPDATE
    AS UPDATE DEPARTMENTS
      SET P_BUDGET = BUDGET
      FROM DEPARTMENTS, INSERTED
      WHERE DEPARTMENTS.DEPT_NO = INSERTED.DEPT_NO
```

This command creates a trigger called UPDATE_BUDGET and tells the DBMS to activate it whenever a row is updated in the DEPARTMENTS table. The trigger itself sets the value of P_BUDGET to the current value of BUDGET for the row where the DEPT_NO value matches the DEPT_NO for the update row (Note the new row values are identified by the INSERTED prefix).

As with DB2's validation procedures, the complexity of triggers means that they usually require a programmer to set them up. Triggers also add a lot of hidden logic to database operations. Seemingly simple SQL commands may have hidden triggers associated with them which may require a lot of additional processing. To a certain extent, this takes away some of the control you have over the database.

7

Views

We've created them, dropped them and used them quite a lot. By now you have a pretty good idea what a database table is and how you can use it store and retrieve information. In this chapter, we will introduce you to another database object (remember that a table is a database object) called the view. Whereas the rows in a table are based on the contents of a physical disk file, the contents of a view are derived from the rows of other tables. In this respect, views are similar to queries in that they too derive a results table based on the contents of other tables. This similarity is more than just coincidence. Views are in fact defined by an SQL query and their contents are the results of executing that query. The difference between queries and views is that views can be queried just like tables. The query defining the view is run (to derive the contents of the view) every time the view becomes the subject of a query.

Figure 7.1 shows the relationship between tables and views. In the rest of this chapter, we will be using the term base tables to refer to the actual SQL tables that you have been using so far and virtual tables to refer to views.

7.1 Restrict the Data You Can See: What is a view?

Most textbooks on the subject like to describe views as windows into base tables. The argument being that views let you look at the table as though through a window. Conceptually, this doesn't make sense. The purpose of a window is to look through it and see the outside world in all its detail. So following on from that, is the idea behind views to look through them and see the contents of the base tables in detail? Not at all. The main point of views is to restrict what you can see of the underlying base tables. The use of views is similar to the use of blinkers. Blinkers are leather sidepieces attached to a horse's bridle which prevent the horse being distracted by side-vision. In the same way, views are applied to tables to prevent users from having access to all the data in the tables. There are four good reasons why we might need to do this.

1. Database security. Views allow you to restrict user's access to only those sections of the database that directly concerns them. In the LECTURERS table for example, you will not want every casual user to be able to access the lecturer's salary information.

2. Data integrity. The DBMS can check the data entered through views to ensure that it meets the conditions defined in the view query.

3. Shielding from change. The view presents a uniform front to the user even if the underlying base table structure is modified, the view can remain constant.

4. Easier querying. Because the view is itself a result of a query, it can reduce complex multi-table queries down to simple SELECT statements.

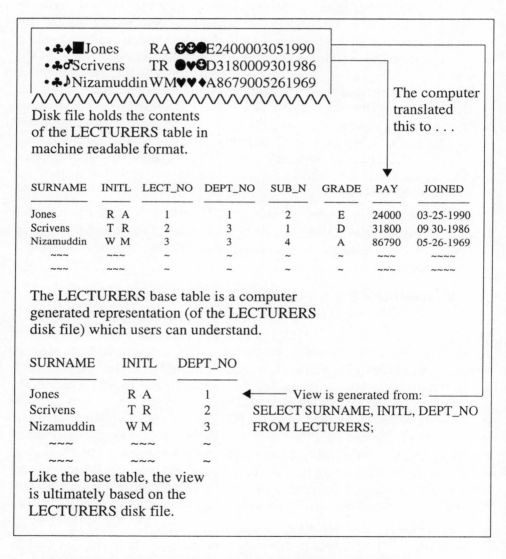

Figure 7.1   How views relate to base tables and disk files

A view cannot be based on more than one query. This means that you are not allowed to use the UNION clause in the view definition (CREATE VIEW) statement.

7.2 How to make Views: The CREATE VIEW command.

Views are created by the CREATE VIEW command. The syntax of this command is shown in Figure 7.2. You can specify the names of the columns for the view if you wish, but it is optional. For example, to restrict users' view of the LECTURERS table to the first five columns only, you could create a view as:

```
CREATE VIEW TEACHING_STAFF
  AS SELECT SURNAME, INITL, LECT_NO, DEPT_NO, SUB_NO
  FROM LECTURERS  ;
  FROM TEACHING_STAFF  ;
```

View TEACHING_STAFF successfully created.

The view is called TEACHING_STAFF and is made up of the first five columns from the LECTURERS table. The names of the columns in the view will be the same as the corresponding columns in the base tables. If as the database administrator, we deny casual users access to the LECTURERS table directly and let them use the view TEACHING_STAFF instead, confidential information such as salary, seniority, grade, etc, will be secure. The view can be queried just like any other table:

CREATE VIEW view_name [**READ ONLY**]
(col_name {, col_name }*)
AS select statement [**WITH CHECK OPTION**] ;

view_name
The name of the view.

col_name
The name of the view's columns. These are optional.

select_statement
The SELECT statement which is used to create the view.

Figure 7.2   The syntax of the Create View command

```
SELECT *
  FROM TEACHING_STAFF ;
```

SURNAME	INITL	LECT_NO	DEPT_NO	SUB_NO
Jones	R A	1	1	2
Scrivens	T R	2	3	1
Nizamuddin	W M	3	3	4
Campbell	J G	4	5	3
Ramanujan	S	5	4	5
Finley	G Y	6	4	5

To look at the contents of the TEACHING_STAFF view, or:

```
SELECT *
  FROM TEACHING_STAFF
  WHERE DEPT_NO = 3 ;
```

SURNAME	INITL	LECT_NO	DEPT_NO	SUB_NO
Scrivens	T R	2	3	1
Nizamuddin	W M	3	3	4

To selectively retrieve rows from the view.

The views we have described so far, allowing access to only certain columns in the tables, are known as vertical views. You can think of them as being made up of vertical slices (columns) of the base table.

Horizontal views as you might have guessed consist of horizontal slices (rows) of data in the table. For example, this command creates a horizontal view which limits access of the STUDENTS table to the rows of first year students only:

```
CREATE VIEW FRESHMEN
  AS SELECT *
  FROM STUDENTS
  WHERE YEAR = 1 ;
```

View FRESHMEN successfully created.

The concept of horizontal and vertical views is not absolute in any way. Indeed, most views are a combination of both. For example, this view, which restricts access to certain columns of first year students in the STUDENTS table is both a horizontal and a vertical view:

```
CREATE VIEW FRESHMEN_2
  AS SELECT SURNAME, FIRST_NAME, DEPT_NO, YEAR
  FROM STUDENTS
  WHERE YEAR = 1 ;
```

View FRESHMEN_2 successfully created.

7.3 Looking through the Window: Using Views

When you query a view, you are in fact performing a query on another query. If we query the FRESHMEN_2 view and retrieve those students who study in department 5 as this query does for example:

```
SELECT *
  FROM FRESHMEN_2
  WHERE DEPT_NO = 5 ;
```

SURNAME	FIRST_NAME	DEPT_NO	YEAR
Layton	Hugh	5	1

then we are in fact looking at those students who are in department 5 and who are also freshmen i.e. whose YEAR column has a value of 1. The query is in effect a combination of the query used to create the view and the query operating on the view. Thus the query on the view can also be expressed in terms of the base table as:

```
SELECT SURNAME, FIRST_NAME, DEPT_NO, YEAR
  FROM STUDENTS
  WHERE YEAR = 1
  AND DEPT_NO = 5 ;
```

SURNAME	FIRST_NAME	DEPT_NO	YEAR
Layton	Hugh	5	1

This combination of view query and the query on the view sometimes leads to problems. For example, this view lists the number of students in each department:

```
CREATE VIEW STUDENT_NUMBERS (DEPT, STUDENTS)
  AS SELECT DEPT_NO, COUNT(*)
  FROM STUDENTS
  GROUP BY DEPT_NO ;
```

View STUDENT_NUMBERS successfully created.

A query on this view to find how many departments have more than 5 students, such as:

```
SELECT *
  FROM STUDENT_NUMBERS
  WHERE STUDENTS > 5 ;
```

Error 67: Aggregate function used in WHERE.

is rejected by SQL. The reason for this is that the combination of the two queries results in an illegal query:

```
SELECT DEPT_NO, COUNT(*)
  FROM STUDENTS
  WHERE COUNT(*) > 5 ;
```

Error 67: Aggregate function used in WHERE.

The STUDENTS column in the view is in fact a calculated column based on COUNT(*). SQL does not allow aggregate functions to be used in a predicate so the query is rejected. If you are not aware of the underlying query used to create the view, then it appears as if SQL has rejected a perfectly legal query.

We listed one of the advantages of using views as leading to easier querying. The chapter on multi-table querying and joins has shown us how complex some SQL queries can get. Views allow you to transfer most of the complex structure of such queries into the view definition itself. Subsequent queries operating on the view will themselves be simple, but the database activity needed to retrieve the results will still be the same. Consider this query which lists the exams taken by students along with the subject and student names. The query implements a three table join:

```
SELECT A.MARK, B.SUB_NAME, C. SURNAME
  FROM EXAMS A, SUBJECTS B, STUDENTS C
  WHERE A.SUB_NO = B.SUB_NO
    AND A.STUDENT_NO = C.STUDENT_NO ;
```

A.MARK	B.SUB_NAME	C.SURNAME
76	Mathamatics	Duke
42	Electronics	Duke
67	Engineering Drwg	Duke
52	English Lit	Al-Essawy
89	English Lit	Ayton
51	English Lit	Ayton
34	Basic Accounts	Patel
49	Marketing	Patel
62	Industrial Law	Jones
70	Industrial Law	Scott
36	Industrial Law	Baker
52	Industrial Law	Brown
67	Organic Chemistry	Monkhouse
82	Organic Chemistry	Grimm
73	Organic Chemistry	Gyver
27	Physiology	Hung-Sun
56	Anatomy	Hung-Sun
67	Anatomy	Middleton
63	Physiology	Middleton

Additional predicate clauses need to be applied to this basic query to selectively retrieve exam records. Such a query is an ideal candidate for a view. To create a view that joins the EXAMS, the SUBJECTS and the STUDENTS table:

```
CREATE VIEW EXAM_MARKS(MARK, SUBJECT, STUDENT)
  AS SELECT A.MARK, B.SUB_NAME, C.SURNAME
    FROM EXAMS A, SUBJECTS B, STUDENTS C
    WHERE A.SUB_NO = B.SUB_NO
      AND A.STUDENT_NO =C.STUDENT_NO ;
```

View EXAM_MARKS successfully created.

It is now a simple matter to query this view. For example, to look at the rows of those students who score more that 70% in their exams, we only have to run this simple query on the EXAM_MARKS view:

```
SELECT *
  FROM EXAM_MARKS
  WHERE MARK > 70 ;
```

MARK	SUBJECT	STUDENT
76	Mathamatics	Duke
89	English Lit	Ayton
82	Organic Chemistry	Grimm
73	Organic Chemistry	Gyver

You are not limited to preforming simple queries on this view. SQL lets you join views to base tables and also to other views, so to look at the marks scored by students from department number 4, we will need to join the EXAM_MARKS view with the STUDENTS base table:

```
SELECT A.SURNAME, A.MARK, B.DEPT_NO
  FROM EXAM_MARKS A, STUDENTS B
  WHERE B.DEPT_NO = 4
    AND A.STUDENT = B.SURNAME ;
```

A.SURNAME	A.MARK	B.DEPT_NO
Duke	76	4
Duke	42	4
Duke	67	4
Al-Essawy	52	4
Baker	36	4
Gyver	73	4

You can also create and use views with subqueries and use views to create other views. This query is an example of both. The ABOVE_AVERAGE view lists the rows from the EXAM_MARKS view where a student's mark is included only if it is greater than the average mark for all exams:

```
CREATE VIEW ABOVE_AVERAGE
AS SELECT MARK, STUDENT, SUBJECT
  FROM EXAM_MARKS A
  WHERE A.MARK >
    (SELECT AVG(B.MARK)
      FROM EXAM_MARKS B) ;
```

View ABOVE_AVERAGE successfully created.

Overall, the ABOVE_AVERAGE view is a result of a lot of DBMS activity but it can be queried just as any other table. Even if we didn't know exactly what it did, we could tell by the name that ABOVE_AVERAGE is going to be a list of values which are greater than the average value of something. This case highlights another important point that you should keep in mind. You should give your queries meaningful names so that it is obvious what the view does. We can tell for example that the ABOVE_AVERAGE view lists the exams where the mark is above the average mark. If we had named it say, EXAMS_VIEW24, then we would need to refer to the CREATE VIEW statement to find out exactly what the view is doing.

7.4 Changing Data Through Views: Updating Views

Updating (remember that this term includes the INSERT, UPDATE and the DELETE statements) data through views can present some problems. Unlike base tables, views allow you to specify aggregate functions as part of the CREATE VIEW definition. By definition, the data in these columns is derived from calculations performed in the base table rows and you will not be able to update data in these columns through the DML commands.

The ANSI/ISO standard specifies that for a view to be updatable, the rows and columns in the view must be directly traceable to the base table that comprise the view. This means that the CREATE VIEW statement must:

- Specify only one base table.

- Not include aggregate functions in the column definitions.

- Not use GROUP BY or HAVING.

- Not use DISTINCT to eliminate duplicate rows from the view.

- Select only simple columns. i.e. expressions, string constants etc. cannot be used.

- Include all the columns from the base table that are defined as NOT NULL.

So the view TEACHING_STAFF is updatable because all its rows relate directly to those of the LECTURERS base table, i.e:

```
UPDATE TEACHING_STAFF
  SET SUB_NO = to  9
  WHERE LECT_NO = 4 ;
```

One row updated.

will change the value of SUB_NO 9 for lecturer number 4. The effect will be the same as performing the UPDATE on the LECTURERS base table itself.

The STUDENT_NUMBERS view on the other hand is not updatable because its definition contains the aggregate function COUNT(*).

7.5 Verifying Data Changes: The WITH CHECK Option

Even if a view is updatable, this does not mean that all updates will be trouble free. One particular problem occurs when you add data to through the view. When a row is added to an updatable view, sometimes, it appears as if the row that you added has gone down a black hole. It is never seen in the view again. Acute observers of SQL queries may already have guessed how this can come about. In order to explain it, let's consider an example. Consider the view:

```
CREATE VIEW LOW_CREDITS
  AS SELECT SUB_NO, SUB-NAME, CREDITS
  FROM SUBJECTS
  WHERE CREDITS = 1 ;
```

View LOW_CREDITS successfully created.

It limits access of the SUBJECTS table to only those subjects where the value for CREDITS is 1. If we now add a row through the view:

```
INSERT INTO LOW_CREDITS
  VALUES (11, 'Geology', 2) ;
```

One row inserted.

The INSERT operation will succeed, but the row won't be visible through the view:

```
SELECT *
  FROM LOW_CREDITS ;
```

No matching records found.

The reason for this is that in the predicate of the CREATE VIEW statement, we specified CREDITS = 1. The value for the CREDITS was 2 in the INSERT. Thus this row will not be accessible through the view even though the row has been entered into the base table. You will not be able to query, update or delete the row via this view.

In order to overcome this problem, SQL allows you to use the WITH CHECK

OPTION clause in the view definition statement. For example, if we had created the LOW_CREDITS view with this option:

```
CREATE VIEW LOW_CREDITS
  AS SELECT SUB_NO, SUB_NAME, CREDITS
  FROM SUBJECTS
  WHERE CREDITS = 1
  WITH CHECK OPTION ;
```

View LOW_CREDITS successfully created.

SQL will now check every INSERT and UPDATE statement that operates on this view against the predicate of the view. If the values in the proposed INSERT conflicts with the predicate of the view, then the command will be rejected. It is always a good idea to use the WITH CHECK OPTION clause in the view definition statement of updatable views as it eliminates the chance of typing errors, etc, from adding rows to the base table which the user will not be able to delete even if he realises the mistake.

7.6   Shutting the Window: The DROP VIEW Command

Views can be deleted from the database by the DROP VIEW command. For example to delete the LOW_CREDITS view:

```
DROP VIEW LOW_CREDITS ;
```

View LOW_CREDITS successfully dropped.

The view will be removed from the database and all queries that reference it will fail. Removal of a view does not affect the underlying base tables or any of the records in them.

8

Database Security

Most SQL based systems operate in a multi-user environment. This means that at any time, several different users can access the same database to query, insert, update or delete data. Such an environment requires safety devices that are built into the DBMS itself and which prevent users from inadvertently corrupting the data. This chapter looks at the security features that are built into SQL itself and also addresses some of the wider aspects of database security.

The DBMS must implement security on two levels. First at the overall database level and second at the individual record level. In this chapter we will be dealing with database security designed to prevent unauthorized access at the overall database level.

8.1   The Term Security is Defined as Protection: SQL Privileges

The term security is defined as protection, defense and safety. In this context, it is a very important aspect of an SQL (or any other) DBMS. Specifically, as part of its security features, the DMBS should protect the data from unauthorized access. It should only allow approved users to use the data in the database and even then, only allow them to perform those functions for which they have authorization.

Without any security features, the data in the database will be accessible by all users. Anyone who felt like it could alter the rows in the tables either inadvertently or maliciously. In almost all organizations, this is not an acceptable state of affairs for a database that might hold vital business and personnel data to be in. Fortunately, the SQL language implements database security as an integral part of its DDL structure.

SQL security is based on the concept of privileges. A privilege can be thought of as permission to perform a certain operation on a certain database object given to a certain user. There are three important concepts here. The first is the privilege which is what we have just described. The second is the idea of database operations which are the actions that you may want to restrict for certain users. Essentially, these operations boil down to queries, insertions, updates and deletions of data. The third is the idea of users who are the people

137

who use the database system and issue SQL commands. The DBMS needs to be aware of everyone who is using the database at any time.

The ANSI/ISO standard defines four privileges that can be granted to or revoked from users: SELECT, INSERT, UPDATE and DELETE. These privileges correspond to the SQL operations that a user is allowed to perform on a given table. The SELECT privilege allows the user to query a table or view. The INSERT privilege allows the user to add rows to a table or view. The DELETE privilege allows the user to delete rows from a table or view and the UPDATE privilege allows the user to modify data in a table or view. Unlike the other three privileges, you can grant UPDATE on selective columns in a table or a view.

8.2   Users Must Introduce Themselves: The Logon Procedure

In order to be able to implement system wide security, the DBMS needs to be aware of exactly who is using the database at any point in time. To do this, almost all commercial SQL DBMSs rely on the concept of authorization-ids. The authorization-id is a label by which SQL identifies each person who is allowed to issue commands to the DBMS (note that a group of users may have similar requirements and may thus share an authorization-id, but is not very common. Usually, each user has his or her own authorization-id). An authorization-id may also be used to identify a program rather than a person that issues SQL commands.

SQL Tips

> SQL Server and Sybase support group-ids which can be used to identify groups of users with similar needs.

New users are registered onto the system by the database administrator who must tell the DBMS to add the new user's authorization-id and password to the list of valid users.

Some commercial SQL implementations, including Ingres and Informix, use the username that is specified in the host computer's logon procedure as the authorization-id for the user. Other systems including Oracle require users to specify the username and also an associated password at the start of the interactive SQL session. The username is used as the authorization-id, but the password is not used in SQL.

SQL Tips

The ANSI/ISO standard uses the term authorization-id instead of user-id.

8.3 The Library Database: An example system

For any table that you create, SQL assigns you as the owner of that table. Ownership of tables means that you automatically have full privileges for that table (these are the four standard ANSI/ISO privileges; SELECT, INSERT, UPDATE and DELETE, already described as well as any other non-ANSI privileges that are supported by your particular dialect of SQL). Initially, all the other users of the database will have no privileges on your new table. Figure 8.1 shows a group of users and the lending library database that they use. The structure of this simple database will be explained as we progress through this chapter.

SQL Tips

The ANSI/ISO standard allows authorization-ids to be up to 18 characters long, but many commercial implementations do not stick to this.

User Frank logs onto the system under the authorization-id FRANK and creates a table called BOOKS by:

```
CREATE TABLE BOOKS  (
    TITLE        CHAR(10),
    AUTHOR       CHAR(15),
    STATUS       CHAR(3)) ;
```

Table books successfully created.

FRANK is now the owner of the BOOKS table. No other user is allowed to access the table. If FRANK adds two rows of data to his table, then SQL accepts this because FRANK has the INSERT privilege on the BOOKS table:

```
INSERT INTO BOOKS
    VALUES ('English', 'U.K.Author', 'IN');
```

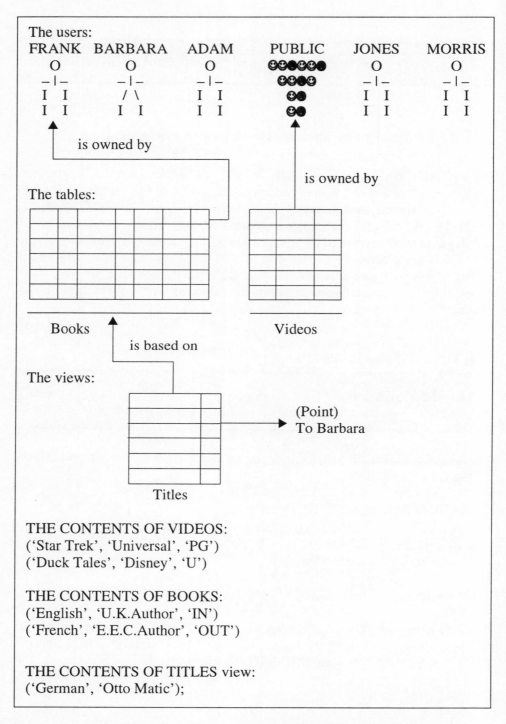

The users:

FRANK   BARBARA   ADAM   PUBLIC   JONES   MORRIS

is owned by

is owned by

The tables:

Books

Videos

is based on

The views:

(Point)
To Barbara

Titles

THE CONTENTS OF VIDEOS:
('Star Trek', 'Universal', 'PG')
('Duck Tales', 'Disney', 'U')

THE CONTENTS OF BOOKS:
('English', 'U.K.Author', 'IN')
('French', 'E.E.C.Author', 'OUT')

THE CONTENTS OF TITLES view:
('German', 'Otto Matic');

Figure 8.1   The tables and users of the lending library database

INSERT INTO BOOKS
  VALUES ('French','E.E.C.Author', 'OUT')

Two rows successfully inserted.

But if user ADAM tries to add a row, then SQL will reject his command because he does not have the necessary privilege:

INSERT INTO BOOKS
  VALUES ('Spanish','E.S.Panya', 'OUT') ;

Error 136: User does not have insert privileges.

Similarly, the VIDEOS table is owned by PUBLIC (this is a special authorization identifier which means that all the users have ownership rights on it), and the view TITLES is owned by BARBARA. Notice that BARBARA doesn't own the BOOKS table on which the view is based.

SQL only lets you create a view, if you have the SELECT privilege on every table used in the view. Ownership of the view will thus guarantee you only the SELECT privilege on it. The other privileges will only be given to you if you already have them for all the base tables used in the view. Thus if you have the INSERT privilege on all of the tables used in the view, then you will also get the INSERT privilege on the view. In the lending library database, user BARBARA must have been granted at least the SELECT and the INSERT privileges on the BOOKS base table in order to be able to create the view and add a row to it.

8.4 How privileges are passed: The GRANT and REVOKE commands

In all the SQL commands used in this book so far, it was assumed that the user was referring to tables that he either owned or ones for which he had been granted the required privileges by the owner of the table. In live database systems, very few users actually own the tables that they query.

SQL Tips

> The ANSI/ISO standard specifies only four privileges for tables and views: Select, insert, update and delete.

Database users are given access to tables, views (collectively known as database objects) and columns by the GRANT statement. This is part of SQL's DDL (data definition language) and is a part of the ANSI/ISO standard. The opposite of GRANT is REVOKE. Privileges that were granted with GRANT are rescinded by the REVOKE command. REVOKE is not included in the ANSI/ISO standard, but is so widely used that it has become almost a de facto standard. The syntax of the GRANT and REVOKE statements is shown in Figures 8.2 and 8.3 respectively.

The table's owner must explicitly grant privileges to all other users who need to use the table. For example, if FRANK wanted to allow BARBARA to be able to query the BOOKS table, then he must grant her the SELECT privilege on BOOKS:

GRANT SELECT ON BOOKS TO BARBARA ;

Privileges successfully granted.

8.4.1   Using views to limit access to columns

The ANSI/ISO standard doesn't allow you to specify columns as arguments to the SELECT privilege command. This means that you must grant SELECT rights for the whole of the table or for none of it. You can get round this

---

GRANT rights **ON** tbl_name **TO** auth_id ;
[WITH GRANT OPTION]

rights
The rights GRANTed may be:
ALL PRIVILEGES |
SELECT | **INSERT** | **UPDATE** | **DELETE**
{ , **SELECT** | **INSERT** | **UPDATE** | **DELETE** }*

tbl_name
The table or view name on which privilege(s) are to be GRANTed.

auth_id The authorization identifier to which privilege(s) are to be GRANTed.

Figure 8.2   The syntax of the GRANT statement

REVOKE rights **ON** tbl_name **FROM** auth_id ;

rights
The rights REVOKEd may be:
ALL PRIVILEGES |
SELECT | INSERT | UPDATE | DELETE
{ , SELECT | INSERT | UPDATE | DELETE }*

tbl_name
The table or view name on which privilege(s) are to be REVOKEd.

auth_id
The authorization identifier from which privilege(s) are to be REVOKEd.

Figure 8.3   The syntax of the REVOKE statement

stipulation by defining a view which only displays the data that you want the user to see and granting him the SELECT privilege on the view and not on the base table. For example, if BARBARA grants ADAM the SELECT privilege on the TITLES view by:

Grant select on titles to Adam ;

Privileges successfully granted.

then ADAM will be able to query the view as much as he likes, but he won't be able to update the data in the view and he won't have any access to the view's base table. SQL will thus reject this query from ADAM:

SELECT *
  FROM BOOKS;

Error 137: User does not have Select privileges.

A serious drawback with using views solely to implement a security structure is the considerable processing overhead that they incur. Indiscriminate use of views can significantly reduce the response time of the overall database.

8.4.2   The ALL PRIVILEGES and PUBLIC keywords

Grant allows you to bestow more than one privilege in a single statement, but does not let you specify more than one authorization-id. Thus FRANK can grant all four privileges to BARBARA on the BOOKS table by:

Grant select, insert, update, delete
  on books
  to Barbara ;

Privileges successfully granted.

Some DBMS have broken from the ANSI/ISO standard and allow you to specify a list of authorization-ids as well as privileges in the GRANT statement. For example, this statement is perfectly legal in DB2's SQL dialect:

Grant select, insert, update, delete on books to Barbara, Morris ;

Privileges successfully granted.

If you want to grant all the available privileges to a user, ANSI/ISO SQL allows you to use the ALL PRIVILEGES clause as a shortcut. So if FRANK wants to give all privileges on the BOOKS table to PUBLIC for example, then he could specify:

Grant all privileges on books to public ;

Privileges successfully granted.

The PUBLIC keyword is a special authorization-id that applies to all users. So the above GRANT statement effectively issues a free for all on the BOOKS table. All users are allowed to perform all operations on BOOKS. This is not a good idea as it means that FRANK now has no control over who is allowed to alter or add data to his table. If an inexperienced user modifies some of the rows without regard to the inter-table relationships that exist, it could easily result in loss of data integrity

SQL Tips

Oracle and IBM's DB2 and SQL/DS support the alter table privilege and a create index privilege.

8.4.3 Selectively granting the **UPDATE** privilege

The SELECT, INSERT and the DELETE privileges, must be either granted for all the columns in a table (or view) or for none of them. The exception to this is the UPDATE privilege. The ANSI/ISO standard allows you to grant the UPDATE privilege selectively for individual columns of a table or view. So in the lending library example, if user ADAM is to be allowed to update the STATUS column of the BOOKS table but not the TITLE or the AUTHOR columns, then FRANK, the owner of the table, can grant this limited update privilege by:

```
GRANT UPDATE (STATUS)
  ON BOOKS
  TO ADAM ;
```

Privileges successfully granted.

Now, ADAM will be able to update the status of books as they are lent out or bought in, but he will not be able to change the values of the TITLE and AUTHOR columns. The column list in UPDATE is optional. If it is omitted, then SQL assumes that the UPDATE privilege is to apply to all the columns. For example, this command gives BARBARA update rights for all columns in the BOOKS table:

```
GRANT UPDATE
  ON BOOKS
  TO BARBARA ;
```

Privileges successfully granted.

8.4.4 Allowing grantees to grant privileges

All the privileges have so far been granted by the owners of the relevant tables and views. But what if a user who himself was granted privileges, a grantee, wants to grant those privileges to other users. The owner can allow this by specifying a WITH GRANT OPTION clause in the initial grant statement. For example, Figure 8.4 shows the chain of privileges that we want to establish. The BOOKS table is owned by FRANK who wants to grant the SELECT privilege on it to BARBARA. User BARBARA in turn wants to grant the SELECT privilege to MORRIS. To accomplish this, FRANK must first grant BARBARA the SELECT privilege:

```
GRANT SELECT
  ON BOOKS
  TO BARBARA
WITH GRANT OPTION ;
```

Privileges succesffuly granted.

BARBARA now has the SELECT privilege on BOOKS. As well as this, the WITH GRANT OPTION lets her grant this privilege to other users as well. Note that the WITH GRANT OPTION only applies to the privileges and the table (or view) named in the GRANT statement. So for example, BARBARA will not be able to grant INSERT or DELETE or UPDATE rights on BOOKS to anyone (how can she, she doesn't have them herself). However, BARBARA can let MORRIS (or anyone else) have the SELECT privilege by:

```
GRANT SELECT
  ON BOOKS
  TO MORRIS ;
```

Privileges successfuly granted.

Now, MORRIS has SELECT privileges on BOOKS as well. If BARBARA had specified WITH GRANT OPTION for MORRIS, it would have allowed MORRIS to grant SELECT rights on BOOKS as well. The original owner of BOOKS, FRANK will know nothing of this chain of privileges propagating through the users, and will in effect have lost charge of the BOOKS table. For tight control of access rights, it is a good idea to be careful about who gets the WITH CHECK option.

8.5   Taking back privileges: The REVOKE statement

All commercial SQL vendors offer the REVOKE command as a method of taking back the privileges that were granted with GRANT. The REVOKE command is in fact an extension to the ANSI/ISO standard. ANSI/ISO SQL includes the GRANT command on the assumption that a database designer will have finalised the design on paper first and then use the DDL commands to create all the tables, views and security privileges. The standard gives the designer a very limited ability to change his mind once the design has been implemented. So under ANSI, once privileges have been assigned, they can only be changed with great difficulty.

SQL Tips

> The REVOKE statement is totally absent from the ANSI/ISO standard.

The format of REVOKE that is implemented by most commercial SQL systems is shown in Figure 8.3. Its format is very similar to the GRANT statement. For example, this command revokes the INSERT and the UPDATE privileges on the TITLES view from MORRIS:

```
REVOKE INSERT, UPDATE
  ON TITLES
  FROM MORRIS ;
```

Privileges successfully revoked.

You can also use the ALL PRIVILEGES clause in the REVOKE command. For example, to stop ADAM using the BOOKS table, FRANK could specify:

```
REVOKE ALL PRIVILEGES
  ON BOOKS
  FROM ADAM ;
```

Privileges successfully revoked.

REVOKE only allows you to rescind those privileges that you yourself granted. This means that if we consider the privilege chain discussed previously and shown in Figure 8.4, FRANK cannot revoke the SELECT privilege on the BOOKS table from MORRIS even though he is the owner of the table. He can however revoke this privilege from BARBARA by:

```
REVOKE SELECT
  ON BOOKS
  FROM BARBARA ;
```

Privileges successfully revoked.

On most systems this will result in the DBMS automatically revoking the corresponding privilege from all the grantees lower down the chain. Thus MORRIS will also lose the SELECT rights on BOOKS as it was granted by BARBARA. As REVOKE is a non-standard feature, different dialects of SQL implement it in subtly different ways. This cascading effect of REVOKE may not be a feature of your particular dialect of SQL.

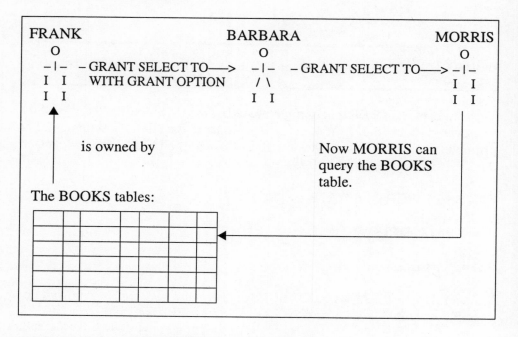

Figure 8.4   A chain of GRANT statements

9

Transaction Processing

Most database updates are implemented by a series of two, three or more individual SQL statements. For example, if a lecturer who is also a Head of a department leaves the university, we would first have to UPDATE the DEPARTMENTS table and set the HEAD field value for the lecturer's department to NULL. Then we would have to delete the lecturer's record from the LECTURERS table. In SQL, this two statement process is called a transaction. The job of this particular transaction is to delete a lecturer's details from the database. Each SQL statement in the transaction performs a part of the overall task, and all the statements must be executed for the database to be in a consistent state.

Complex transactions can involve five or six update (remember this includes INSERT, UPDATE and DELETE) statements and if some of them are executed by the DBMS and for some reason the others are not, the data integrity of the data will be lost. To guard against this, SQL provides a way of reversing the effects of commands that modify data so if a crash does occur in the middle of a transaction, the partially completed transaction can be discarded and the database data returned to its initial state before the transaction was run.

9.1 A Transaction as a Fundamental Unit of Work: The COMMIT and ROLLBACK commands

The DBMS must ensure that a transaction is treated as a fundamental unit of work. This means that once the DBMS has started processing the first statement in a transaction, it must carry on until all the remaining statements are also processed, the transaction cannot be half-processed. All the statements in the transaction must be treated as a single unit.

If processing is halted in the middle of a transaction, as a result of a re-boot or a system crash for example, then the DBMS must reverse the state of the database to that which existed before the transaction was started. The special SQL command to do this is ROLLBACK. If all the statements in the transaction are successfully executed, then the database changes are made permanent by the COMMIT command. COMMIT and ROLLBACK are regular ANSI/ISO

149

standard SQL statements, like SELECT, INSERT, etc, that can be used in both programmatic and interactive SQL. The ANSI/ISO standard specifies that transaction processing must always be in effect. It starts with the start of the interactive SQL session or the user program and ends with either a COMMIT command, a ROLLBACK command, the termination of the user program or a catastrophic system crash.

9.1.1 A practical example of transaction processing

You will understand the ideas behind transactions and the need for them by looking at a practical example. Figure 9.1 shows an invoice processing system. The two tables represent two sections of an invoice. The INV_HEADER table is the invoice header which holds the details of invoice number, the customer number who the invoice is made out to, the date of invoice and the total number of items that have been ordered. The INV_BODY table holds such details as the items that appear on the invoice. It has fields for invoice number, the quantity

INVOICE_NO	CUST_NUM	DATE	ITEMS	
~~	~~~	~~~	~~	
~~	~~~	~~~	~~	The invoice header table.
345	234	7-AUG-92	88	
456	453	6-SEP-92	71	
234	687	5-APR-92	57	
~~	~~~	~~~	~~	
~~	~~~	~~~	~~	

INV_HEADER

INVOICE_NO	QTY	DESCRIPTION	VALUE	
~~	~~~	~~~~~~~~~	~~~	
~~	~~~	~~~~~~~~~	~~~	
~~	~~~	~~~~~~~~~	~~~	
345	25	DC POWER SPPLY	5500	The invoice body table.
345	18	SERIAL I/O CRD	1500	
345	45	SVGA CARDS	2780	
234	57	486 CPUs	6745	
~~	~~~	~~~~~~~~~	~~~	
~~	~~~	~~~~~~~~~	~~~	

INV_BODY

Figure 9.1   An invoice processing system

of each item, the description of the item and the total value of the items. As each order is received, the staff must add a row to the INV_HEADER table for the new invoice, and rows to the INV_BODY table for the items ordered. A customer can ask for several different items in a single order, so each row of INV_HEADER can have several associated rows in the INV_BODY table.

Figure 9.2 shows how a new order is added to the invoicing system. Without any transaction processing, the rows in INV_HEADER and INV_BODY can get into an inconsistent state. For example, if SQL succeeds in adding an invoice header row to INV_HEADER, but fails in inserting all the items into INV_BODY, the ITEMS figure in INV_HEADER will not equal the sum of the

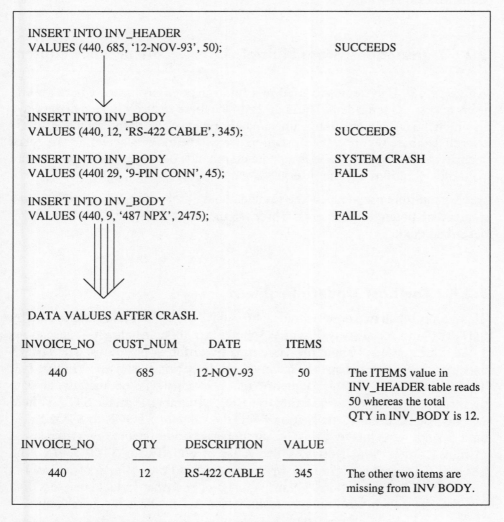

Figure 9.2 Adding a new order to the invoicing system

QTY values in INV_BODY. It will be worse still if we add the items first and then the header. SQL may succeed in adding the items, but fail to insert the header row. We will then have rows of items that have no corresponding invoice header record.

With transaction processing in effect, if the system fails or the program crashes, you can discard the half completed transaction with a ROLLBACK statement. In Figure 9.2, ROLLBACK would remove the two INSERTs that succeeded and revert the database to the state that it was in before the transaction was started. You can then re-run the whole transaction again and if SQL succeeds in executing all the statements, make the INSERTs permanent by issuing the COMMIT command.

9.2   Transactions From Multiple Users: Concurrency control

Almost all SQL systems are used in a multi-user environment where several users access the same data. The chapter on database security looked at the ways in which the DBMS ensures against unauthorized access to the database, this is overall database security. In this section, we will be looking at another aspect of security; ensuring that the SQL update commands of one user do not interfere with the operations of other users.

Having multiple users access the same database at the same time can lead to a number of potential problems. Three of the most well known of these are described next.

9.2.1   The Lost Update Problem

This occurs when two or more transactions have their statements interleaved by the DBMS in a certain way. Figure 9.3 shows how this can happen. Transactions 1 and 2 are started at about the same time by different programs. The DBMS executes the individual statements in each transaction as shown in Figure 9.3. The overall result of this sequence of operations will be that the update performed by the Order Processing transaction (number 1) on the STOCK field will be lost. At time=1, transaction 1 sets the value of STOCK to STOCK-10, but does not write this to disk. The computer allocates the next two time slices to transaction 2 which updates the value of STOCK to STOCK+75. The STOCK value that is eventually written to disk (at time=4) by transaction 1 is the value set by transaction 2. Transaction 1's update has in fact been lost. In a live database, such 'lost' updates result in serious database inconsistency.

TRANSACTION 1   (Order Processing)
_____

READ STOCK VALUE
SET STOCK = STOCK-10
WRITE STOCK VALUE
READ QTY VALUE
SET QTY = QTY+10
WRITE QTY VALUE

TRANSACTION 2   (Goods Received)
_____

READ STOCK VALUE
SET STOCK = STOCK+75
WRITE STOCK VALUE

Two programs run these transactions at about the same time. Transaction 1 is a part of the new order processing program and transaction 2 is a part of the stock control system for goods received.

The DBMS might execute these transaction statements in the following order:

TIME	STATEMENT	TRANSACTION No.
0	READ STOCK VALUE	Order Proc. (1)
1	SET STOCK = STOCK-10	Order Proc. (1)
2	READ STOCK VALUE	Goods Recv. (2)
3	SET STOCK = STOCK+75	Goods Recv. (2)
4	WRITE STOCK VALUE	Order Proc. (1)
5	READ QTY VALUE	Order Proc. (1)
6	WRITE STOCK VALUE	Goods Recv. (2)
7	SET QTY = QTY+10	Order Proc. (1)
8	WRITE QTY VALUE	Order Proc. (1)

At time=6, transaction 2 has written an incorrect value because the update by transaction 1 has been lost.

Figure 9.3   The lost update problem in concurrent transactions

9.2.2   The Temporary Update Problem

This problem occurs when one transaction updates a table row and then cancels the update with ROLLBACK. The temporarily updated row can be accessed by another transaction before it is changed back to its original value. Figure 9.4 shows the sequence of operations that can cause the temporary update problem. Transaction 1 sets the value of STOCK to STOCK-10 and writes this to disk. The DBMS then starts transaction 2 which reads the value of STOCK which has just been updated by transaction 1. This value is set to STOCK+75 and written to disk by transaction 2. When control is given back to transaction 1, it issues a ROLLBACK command (as a result of program crash for example) and cancels the STOCK = STOCK-10 update. This means that the value for STOCK read by transaction 2 at time=3 was incorrect. It had in fact read the temporary value. As with the lost update problem, the temporary update problem will also result in database inconsistency if left unchecked.

9.2.3 The incorrect summary problem

This is the third common problem that can occur when multiple transactions operate on the data without any form of concurrency control by the DBMS. It is illustrated in Figure 9.5. Transaction 4 is part of a report generating program. It

---

The statements in the transactions are as described in Figure 9.3.

The DBMS might execute these transaction statements in the following order:

TIME	STATEMENT	TRANSACTION No.
0	READ STOCK VALUE	Order Proc. (1)
1	SET STOCK = STOCK-10	Order Proc. (1)
2	WRITE STOCK VALUE	Order Proc. (1)
3	READ STOCK VALUE	Goods Recv. (2)
4	SET STOCK = STOCK+75	Goods Recv. (2)
5	WRITE STOCK VALUE	Goods Recv. (2)
6	READ QTY VALUE	Order Proc. (1)
7	ROLLBACK	Order Proc. (1)

Transaction 1 fails at time=7 and resets the STOCK field to its original value. Transaction 2 has therefore read the temporary, incorrect value of STOCK at time=3.

Figure 9.4   The temporary update problem in concurrent transactions

TRANSACTION 3   (Order Processing)

READ STOCK VALUE
SET STOCK = STOCK-10
WRITE STOCK VALUE
READ STOCK VALUE
READ QTY VALUE
SET STOCK = STOCK+QTY
WRITE STOCK VALUE

TRANSACTION 4   (Total Stock)

SUM(STOCK) FOR
ALL ITEMS

Two programs run these transactions at about the same time. Transaction 3 is a part of the new order processing program and transaction 2 is a part of a report generation program that calculates the sum of the STOCK row values.

The DBMS might execute these transaction statements in the following order:

TIME	STATEMENT	TRANSACTION No.
0	SUM=0;	Total Stok. (4)
1	READ STOCK (rowl)	Total Stok. (4)
2	SUM=SUM+STOCK (rowl)	Total Stok. (4)
3	READ STOCK (row2)	Order Proc. (3)
4	SET STOCK = STOCK-10 (row2)	Order Proc. (3)
5	WRITE STOCK VALUE (row2)	Order Proc. (3)
6	READ STOCK (row2)	Total Stok. (4)
7	SUM=SUM+STOCK (row2)	Total Stok. (4)
8	READ STOCK (row3)	Total Stok. (4)
9	SUM=SUM+STOCK (row3)	Total Stok. (4)
10	READ STOCK (row3)	Order Proc. (3)
11	READ QTY VALUE	Order Proc. (3)
12	SET STOCK = STOCK+QTY (row3)	Order Proc. (3)
13	WRITE STOCK VALUE (row3)	Order Proc. (3)

Transaction 4 reads the value of STOCK (row2), at time=6, after transaction 3 has subtracted 10 from it. At time=8, transaction 4 reads STOCK (row3) before transaction 3 subtracts QTY. The sum of the STOCK field values will thus be off by the value of QTY.

Figure 9.5   The incorrect summary problem in concurrent transactions

reads the value of the STOCK column for each row in the table and adds up the sum total. Transaction 3 is part of the order processing program that handles returned products. The problem occurs when the summing transaction reads and adds a value of a row after the order processing transaction has changed its value for one row (at time=6) and before the order processing transaction has added the value of QTY for the next row (at time=8). It results in the sum total calculated by transaction 4, being off by an amount equal to the value of QTY from the actual sum of the STOCK column values. The incorrect summary problem won't cause inconsistencies in the database, but will give unreliable results in the reports. Not very good for basing important corporate decisions on.

9.2.4   Data Locking

The three possible problems just described force the DBMS to implement some kind of mechanism that prevents the updates of multiple users from interfering with each other and from corrupting the data in the database. The DBMS must make sure that the data in the database is consistent throughout each transaction and that it is unaffected by transient changes made by other concurrently running transactions. The DBMS does this by not allowing concurrent transactions to access the same rows of data at the same time. Once a transaction accesses a row in the database, the DBMS doesn't allow any other transaction to modify that row (they can only read it). This is done through a technique called locking and is applied automatically by the DBMS. It is totally transparent to the SQL user.

There are two basic types of locks that are used by most SQL DBMS. The share lock and the exclusive lock. Share locks allow multiple transactions to access the data that the lock is applied to but do not allow transactions to modify it. Share locks can be applied by more than one transaction to the same data. The second type of basic lock is the exclusive lock. Exclusive locks can only be applied by one transaction at a time, and prevent all other users from locking the same data. Exclusive locks are applied when transactions want to update data in the database and share locks are applied when transactions want to read the data. The rules for applying share and exclusive locks is shown in Figure 9.6.

When you access rows of data through a transaction, the DBMS prevents other users from modifying those rows while your transaction is still running. So if you run a SELECT that accesses lots of rows from a table, no other user will be able to change the values of those rows while your transaction is processing. This is why you should keep your transactions as short as possible to maximize concurrent transaction activity in the database.

Although locking prevents the problems associated with concurrent transactions which we have described i.e. lost update problem, temporary update problem,

		Transaction 1		
		NO LOCK	SHARE LOCK	EXCLUSIVE LOCK
T r a n s a c t i o n 2	NO LOCK	yes	yes	yes
	SHARE LOCK	yes	yes	no
	EXCLUSIVE LOCK	yes	no	no

Figure 9.6   Rules for applying share and exclusive locks

TRANSACTION 1   (T1)

UPDATE STUDENTS ROW 3
UPDATE EXAMS ROW 7

TRANSACTION 2   (T2)

UPDATE EXAMS ROW 7
UPDATE STUDENTS ROW 3

x-lock = Exclusive lock.
s-lock = Share lock.

The DBMS runs these two transactions as:

TIME	STATEMENT	TRANSACTION	LOCK APPLIED
0	UPDATE STUDENTS ROW 3	T1	x-lock on row3 students.
1	UPDATE EXAMS ROW 7	T2	x-lock on row7 exams.
2	UPDATE EXAMS ROW 7	T1	none, Transaction Waits.
3	UPDATE STUDENTS ROW 3	T2	none, Transaction Waits.

Transaction 1 is waiting for the row locked by transaction 2 to be released and transaction 2 is waiting for the row locked by transaction 1 to be released. They will both wait forever, i.e. they are in a deadlock.

Figure 9.7   A deadlock situation

etc, they introduce another potential problem called a deadlock. This is illustrated in Figure 9.7. Transaction 1 updates the STUDENTS table first then updates the EXAMS table. Transaction 2 does the same thing, but the other way round. If the transactions are executed by the DBMS as shown, transaction 1 updates a part of the STUDENTS table and locks the part of it that it accesses. Transaction 2 then updates the EXAMS table and locks part of that. Now each transaction is trying to update part of the table that has been locked by the other transaction. The transactions are deadlocked. See Figure 9.7. Such deadlocks can also occur between three or more transactions and without external intervention, each transaction will wait forever.

The DBMS handles deadlocks by periodically checking for them. If a deadlock is detected, one of the transactions is arbitrarily chosen as the deadlock loser and is rolled back thereby releasing the deadlock. This means that any transaction could be rolled back by the DBMS at any time because it resulted in a deadlock with another transaction. In interactive SQL, this is not much of a problem. All it means is that you will have to re-enter the whole transaction again.

10

The Database System Catalog

In a working SQL database, the DBMS needs to keep track of tables, columns, views, authorization-ids and privileges. Most commercial systems rely on special relational database tables called the system catalog for this. The system catalog or system tables consist of tables that are created and owned by the DBMS itself. The DBMS does not allow anyone to modify or add data to these tables, but on most systems, users can query them and obtain information on tables, views, other users, etc.

The system catalog is not defined in the ANSI/ISO standard, in fact, the standard does not specify how SQL DBMSs should maintain the database at all. As a result of this, this area is the most diverse amongst the commercial SQL based DBMSs. Although all the major vendors have chosen to use the system catalog to administer the database, they all differ in the implementation details. This chapter describes the structure and content of a typical system catalog by looking at the system tables of some popular commercial SQL DBMSs.

10.1 The DBMS Needs to Manage its Resources: A typical system catalog

Although the various commercial SQL systems offer widely varying features, they all have a common base of resources that the DBMS needs to manage as a minimum requirement. These are shown in Figure 10.1. They include:

1. Tables. All the tables in the database must be known to the DBMS. The information must include the table's name and the table's owner.

2. Views. These are related to tables and indeed, some system catalogs have a single table that stores details of both tables and views. Typically, the DBMS needs to know the view's name, its owner and the defining query.

3. Columns. The DBMS must know details of all columns for both tables and views. Typical information includes the column name, the table or view which the column is part of and the data type and size of the column.

4. Users. Each user has an associated authorization-id. The DBMS needs to

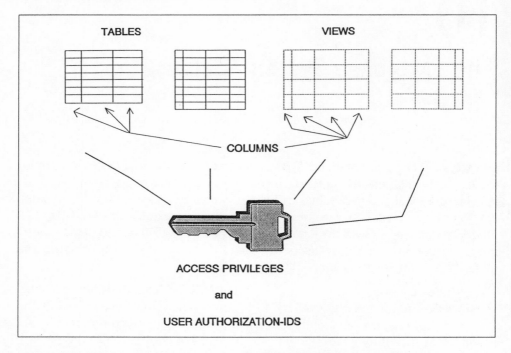

Figure 10.1   The resources that a typical SQL DBMS must manage

keep track of all the authorization-ids as well as the passwords that they are identified by.

5. Privileges. The DBMS needs to be aware of the privileges that have been granted. Specifically, it needs to know the authorization-id of the grantor, and the grantee, the privilege that has been granted and the table/view that the privilege was granted on.

All this information is itself stored in relational database tables. Most systems use a different table for each of the five categories listed above.

SQL Tips

> The ANSI/ISO standard does not specify any form of database regulation
> . Almost all commercial systems rely on the system catalog for this.

10.1.1 Table information in the system catalog

The system table that keeps track of the details of all other tables in the database is called SYSTABLES in IBM's OS/2 EE. The table is owned by the DBMS itself so to query it, you must use the SYSIBM prefix. For example to list the names of all the tables and views in the database along with the owner and the number of columns, an OS/2 EE query would be:

```
SELECT NAME, CREATOR, COLCOUNT
  FROM SYSISM.SYSTABLES ;
```

Note that NAME, CREATOR, COLCOUNT and TYPE are all fields in the SYSTABLES system table where NAME is the name of the table or view. CREATOR is the owner of the object. COLCOUNT is a number specifying the number of columns in the object and TYPE is either T for tables or V for views. SYSTABLES can be queried just like any other table, and stores its information as other tables, in rows and columns. For example it has multiple columns and one row of data for each table or view in the database. You could also add a predicate to your query, as you would for any other query, to list only the tables that are owned by FRANK for example:

```
SELECT NAME, CREATOR, COLCOUNT
  FROM SYSIBM.SYSTABLES
  WHERE TYPE = 'T'
  AND CREATOR = 'FRANK' ;
```

10.1.2 View information in the system catalog

Some systems include basic information on views with the tables and store them both in a system objects table. IBM's OS/2 EE for example has a TYPE column in SYSTABLES to distinguish between tables and views. Other information relating directly to views is stored in different tables. OS/2 EE has two further system catalog tables that hold information on views. The SYSVIEWS table holds the SQL text information that defines the view. The SYSVIEWDEP table holds the details of the base tables (and views) that the view derives its information from. You can also query these like ordinary tables. For example to list the base tables/views and their owners which the MGRS view depends on:

```
SELECT BNAME, BCREATOR, BTYPE
  FROM SYSIBM.SYSVIEWDEP
  WHERE DNAME = 'MGRS' ;
```

BNAME holds the name of a table/view on which the view depends. BCREATOR holds the name of the owner and BTYPE is either 'T' for tables and 'V' for views. DNAME is the column that holds the name of the dependent view. SYSVIEWDEP has one row for each base object. So if the MGRS view has three tables in its definition, there will be three rows in SYSVIEWDEP with a DNAME value of 'MGRS'.

10.1.3   Column information in the system catalog

Just keeping details of tables and views is not enough to manage a database. The DBMS also needs to know about all the columns in each table and view. All the major commercial SQL DBMSs use a system catalog table to keep track of columns. IBM's OS/2 EE for example uses the SYSCOLUMNS table for this. This table holds the information directly relating to the column such as the column name, data type, the table or view it is part of, etc, as well as statistical information which the DBMS uses to optimize queries which access the column. This information is generally of no use to us directly, but we can query SYSCOLUMNS to extract useful information. For example, to find the number of columns and their types in the LECTURERS table:

```
SELECT NAME, COLTYPE, LENGTH
  FROM SYSIBM.SYSCOLUMNS
  WHERE TBNAME = 'LECTURERS' ;
```

NAME, COLTYPE and LENGTH are fields in SYSCOLUMNS which hold details of the name of the column, its data type and its size respectively. TBNAME stores the name of the table which the column is part of.

10.1.4   User information in the system catalog

Knowledge of all valid authorization-ids is essential if the DBMS is going to maintain system security. Information on users is stored in a table in the system catalog. There is usually one row per user in this table. Typical details that are stored include the authorization-id and the associated password for each user. The nature of this information is such that sensitive information such as user passwords is only available to database administrators and users who have very high security clearance.

10.1.5   Privileges information in the system catalog

The privileges information table holds the details of the privileges granted to users. Typically, the DBMS stores details such as the privilege granted, the user who granted the privilege, the user who received the privilege, the database object to which the privilege applies, a time stamp to indicate when the privilege was granted, etc. Whenever a user enters an SQL statement, the DBMS first check if that user has the required privileges to carry out the task.

10.1.6   Commenting the tables, views and columns

In large, complex databases, it can become difficult to remember the exact functions of all the tables, views and columns. Although there is no substitute for thorough design documentation, most commercial SQL systems also allow you to attach labels and comments to each table, view and column defined in the database. The remarks are usually stored in the system catalog's objects definition table, e.g. SYSTABLES. Labels are attached by using the LABEL statement. Thus to add a label to the EXAMS table:

```
LABELS ON TABLE EXAMS
  IS 'The exams taken by the students'
```

The label is stored with the table definition in the system catalog. You can also attach labels to the individual columns. For example, to label the BUDGET column in the DEPARTMENTS table:

```
LABEL ON COLUMN DEPARTMENTS.BUDGET
  IS 'Internally allocated budget.' ;
```

LABEL is used to attach a short descriptive label to a table or column. The COMMENT statement lets you add a longer description to the SYSTABLES row for the table or view or the SYSCOLUMNS row for the column. For example, to add a remark to the GRADE column in the LECTURERS table:

```
COMMENT ON LECTURERS
  (GRADE IS 'Grade A is the most senior and E, the most junior')
```

The remark is stored in the SYSCOLUMNS table and is appended to the row for the GRADE column. You should add labels and remarks for all but the very simplest of database tables. This is because when you or someone else refers to the structure of the database in a few months time say, comments are an invaluable aid in finding out exactly what information the columns store and how the inter-table relationships are formed.

11

Embedding SQL in a Host Language

The SQL language as we have used it so far has been used as an interactive database query language. All the queries have been typed in at the system prompt and the DBMS executed each query and output the results immediately (or at least, while we waited!). This is fine for ad hoc queries that will not be repeated or are run infrequently. Almost all commercial SQL systems provide this type of interface called either interpretive SQL or interactive SQL. This chapter looks at the other method of using SQL, programmatic SQL.

The term programmatic SQL is used to refer to SQL statements that are used in conjunction with another computer language called the host language.

11.1 SQL is not a Computer Programming Language: Why SQL needs a host language

By itself, SQL is a very powerful query language. However, it is not a computer programming language in the real sense of the word. For instance, it does not have any commands that enable programs to loop or branch to different sections of the program code, such as FOR, DO..WHILE and IF..THEN statements. In programmatic SQL, these are provided by a host language such as Pascal, C, FORTRAN or COBOL.

There are basically two distinct methods of interfacing SQL with a host language. One is embedded SQL and the other is through an application program interface (API). Embedded SQL is concerned with mixing SQL statements directly with the host language code. Embedded SQL is the subject of this chapter. The application program interface or API is a library of DBMS functions through which the host language program issues commands to the DBMS. The API appears to the host language program as just another library which the linker can link into the program.

Originally, the ANSI/ISO standard supported programmatic SQL through the concept of modules. These are SQL procedures which must be called from a separate module language program. The standard was extended in 1989 to

165

include embedded SQL in the COBOL, FORTRAN, C, PL/1, Pascal and Ada host languages.

11.2 How Embedded SQL Programs are Processed: Compile, Bind and Link

Figure 11.1 shows a short embedded SQL program written in the C language. The SQL statements are highlighted for clarity. Don't worry too much if you do not fully understand how the program operates, we will be discussing it fully in the next few sections.

When this program is run, it asks the user for a department number. The program then runs an SQL query which fetches the row from the DEPARTMENTS table that the department number applies to, and displays the department name and the current year's budget. The output from the program is shown in Figure 11.2.

Although we have chosen to write in C, other languages such as Pascal, COBOL, etc, would have been just as applicable.

The embedded SQL program, such as the one in Figure 11.1 cannot be directly compiled by the C compiler because of the embedded SQL statements. Figure 11.3 shows the steps involved in converting the embedded SQL source code (shown in Figure 11.1) into an executable embedded SQL program.

The sequence of operations that are illustrated in Figure 11.3 are invisible to the program developer. Typically, the developer is only required to start the process with a single command. This is not so different from 'normal' program development, where you would start off the compile and link process with a single MAKE command. Even though the whole process is initiated by a single command, it follows distinct stages:

1. The embedded SQL program is passed to a precompiler. A precompiler is a software tool provided by the SQL system vendors. It separates the embedded SQL program code into a host language program file and the SQL statements stored in a file called the database request module (DBRM).

2. The host language file from the precompiler is submitted to the standard language compiler for compilation into an object file.

3. The compiled object files from the compiler are then submitted to the linker and linked with any library routines that may be required.

4. The DBRM file from the precompiler is operated upon by a binding program which produces an application plan for all the SQL statements. This plan tells the DBMS all it needs to know about accessing the data in the database requested by the SQL statements. The application plan is stored in the database.

```
main ( )
{
    exec sql include sqlca;
    exec sql begin declare section;
        int    input_val;              /* User input */
        int    d_no;                   /* Department Number */
        char   d_name [21];            /* Department Name */
        int    d_head;                 /* Departmental Head */
        float  budget;                 /* Current Budget */
        float  p_budget;               /* Previous Budget */
    exec sql end declare section;

    /* SQL' s error condition handling */
    exec sql whenever sqlerror goto error_handler;
    exec sql whenever not found goto no_number;

    /* Ask the user for a department number */
    printf ( "Enter the department number : " );      /* Prompt */
    scanf ( "%d", &input_val);                        /* Read Input */

    /* SQL query to retrive a record. */
    exec sql select dept_no, dept name, head, budget, p_budget
                from departments
                where dept_no = :input val
                into :d_no, :d_name, :d_head, :budget, :p_budget;

    /* Now output some results */
    printf ( "Department name       :  %s\n", d_name);
    printf ( "Current year' s budget :  %f\n", budget);

    /* Error Handling */
error_handler:
    printf ( "DBMS error occurred, code : %ld\n", sqlca . sqlcode);
    exit ( );

    /* Row Not Found Handling */
no_number:
    printf ( " %d is an invalid Department number\n", input_val);
exit ( );
}
```

Figure 11.1   An embedded SQL program in the C language

The user input is shown in bold.

Enter the department number : **5**
Department name   : Physical Sciences
Current year's budget : 4680000

Figure 11.2   The Embedded SQL program operation.

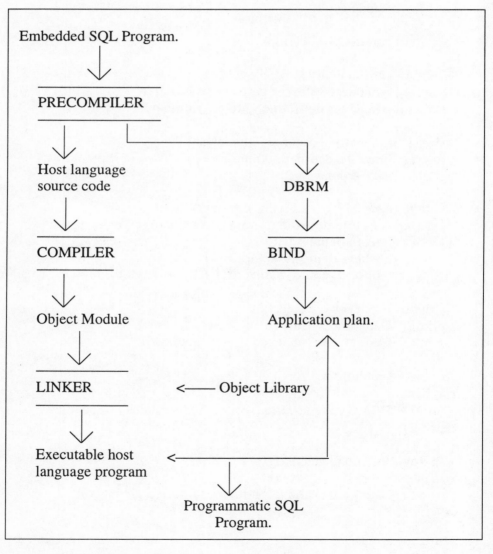

Figure 11.3   Embedded SQL program development

By the end of these stages, the host language part of the program is compiled and linked and the SQL part is parsed, validated and optimised.

When the program is run, the executable host language program will be loaded and executed as any other program. Whenever the program needs to execute an SQL statement, it instructs the DBMS to find and load the application plan for that statement. The main program and the DBMS thus co-operate to run the whole embedded SQL program.

11.3 How SQL Statements Are Embedded: The EXEC SQL clause

In the embedded SQL program of Figure 11.1, the SQL statements are preceded by the "exec sql" precompiler directive. This introducer tells the precompiler that the next statement is an SQL command. The statement ends with a terminator. In C, this is the semicolon character. Other languages use other terminators, for example, COBOL uses END-EXEC. Although the C language is case sensitive (printf is not the same as Printf), the SQL statement after EXEC SQL can be either upper or lower case. This is because these statements are removed by the precompiler before they reach the C compiler so the compiler does not see them directly.

11.4 How SQL Talks to the Host Language: Host language variables

Host language variables are used to supply values or receive values from SQL. The variables should first be declared in the program using the ANSI/ISO standard BEGIN DECLARE SECTION and END DECLARE SECTION statements. For example, in the program listed in Figure 11.1, the host language variables that are going to be used with SQL are declared as:

```
exec sql begin declare section;
      int   input_val;              /* User input */
      int   d_no;                   /* Department Number */
      char  d_name[21];             /* Department Name */
      int   d_head;                 /* Departmental Head */
      float budget;                 /* Current Budget */
      float p_budget;               /* Previous Budget */
exec sql end declare section;
```

The host language variables must be compatible with the SQL data types which they refer to. For example, SQL's INTEGER type corresponds to C's int type and SQL's CHARACTER type is compatible with C's char type. Sometimes, there will not be an exact match e.g. the BUDGET field is DECIMAL and the closest match in C is the float type.

Once they have been declared, the host language variables can be used in the SQL statements, preceded by a colon. For example:

```
exec sql select dept_no, dept_name, head, budget, p_budget
        from departments
        where dept_no = :input_val
        into :d_no, :d_name, :d_head, :budget, :p_budget;
```

This SELECT statement is the programmatic SELECT which has an additional INTO clause. The variables specified in this clause are the host language variables declared earlier. The values from the fields specified in the SELECT clause are retrieved into the host language variables. These can then be used in the rest of the program as normal.

Keen observers might have spotted a problem that can occur with the SELECT INTO statement. What happens if the query retrieves more than one row? The short answer to this is that it can't. If the query retrieves more than one row, then all the values cannot be placed in the host language variables and the query will fail. This restriction only applies to the SELECT INTO statement. It is possible to use queries that fetch multiple rows in programmatic SQL by using a data object known as a cursor. This is described in the next section.

11.5 Handling Queries That Retrieve Multiple Rows: The SQL cursor

SELECT INTO can only be used with queries that output a single row. For the majority of queries, which retrieve multiple rows, you must use a cursor to access the results table of the query. A cursor is a logical object that is associated with a particular query. This is similar to a view which is associated with a particular query and which derives its contents by running the query.

11.5.1 Selects with cursors

Figure 11.4 shows an embedded SQL program which uses a cursor. As before, the SQL statements are shown highlighted for clarity.

The cursor must be declared first before it can be used. In the program of Figure 11.4, this is done by:

```
main ( )
{
    exec sql include sqlca;
    exec sql begin declare section;
        int     d_no;                   /* Department Number */
        char    d_name [21];            /* Department Name */
        int     d_head;                 /* Departmental Head */
        float   budget;                 /* Current Budget */
        float   p_budget;               /* Previous Budget */
    exec sql end declare section;

    /* Decalare a cursor */
    exec sql declare dptcurs cursor for
        select dept_no, dept_name, head, budget
            from departments
            where dept_no < 10 ;

    /* SQL's error condition handling */
    exec sql whenever sqlerror goto error handler;
    exec sql whenever not found goto no more rows;

    /* Open the cursor */
    exec sql_open dptcurs ;

    /* Output results of the query by looping */
    printf ("Dept No.      Dept Name      Head      Budget\n" );
    printf (" ———          ————           ——        ——\n" );

    do {
        /* Get the next row of results */
            exec sql fetch dptcurs
                    into :d_no, :d_name, :d_head, :budget ;

    /* Now display the row data */
    printf ( "%d\t %s\t %d\t %f\n", d_no, d_name, d_head, budget );
    } while(l) ;

    /* Error Handling */
error_handler:
    printf ( "DBMS error occurred, code : %ld\n", sqlca . sqlcode); exit ( );

    /* Row Not Found Handling */
no_more_rows:
    puts ( "\n\t\tNo more Rows . " );
    /* Release the resources held by the cursor */
    exec sql close dptcurs ;
    exit ( );

}
```

Figure 11.4   Embedded SQL program using a cursor

```
exec sql declare dptcurs cursor for
  select dept_no, dept_name, head, budget
    from departments
    where dept_no < 10 ;
```

The cursor is named as 'dptcurs' and is assigned to the query shown. This query is not executed immediately, it is only used to define the cursor at this stage.

In order to actually execute the query, you must open the cursor. For example:

```
exec sql open dptcurs ;
```

This statement causes the query associated with the cursor called dptcurs to be executed. The results of the query can be accessed by the FETCH statement. In the program of Figure 11.4, this is done by:

```
exec sql fetch dptcurs
         into :d_no, :d_name, :d_head, :budget ;
```

The FETCH statement retrieves the first row from the results table into the host language variables specified and sets the row pointer to point to the next row in the results. We placed the FETCH statement in a repeating loop because it retrieves the next row from the results each time it is run. The do..while loop continues to fetch results and display them until no more rows are left to be fetched. When FETCH reaches the end of the results table, it causes the program to jump to the "no_more_rows" label where a "No more rows" message is output. Note that although you can move down through the results table by using the FETCH command, there is no way of moving up through the results table. This means that when all the rows have been fetched through a cursor, it must be closed. There is no point in tying up system resources in maintaining an exhausted cursor. The CLOSE CURSOR command releases the resources allocated to the cursor, for example:

```
exec sql close dptcurs ;
```

To use the dptcurs cursor again, you must be re-declare it and then open it. The output of this program is shown in Figure 11.5

11.5.2 Deletes and Updates with cursors

You can use cursors to delete and update data in SQL tables. Cursors by themselves can only access data through a query. They cannot therefore be

Dept No.	Dept Name	Head	Budget
1	Engineering	59	5780000
2	Arts & Humanities	23	753000
3	Management Studies	3	2510000
4	Industrial Law	12	78000
5	Physical Sciences	18	4680000
6	Medicine	67	6895000

No more Rows.

Figure 11.5   Output of the cursor based query program

directly used with a DELETE statement. However, programmatic SQL allows the use of a DELETE statement with WHERE CURRENT OF clause which uses a cursor to specify the row to delete.

Figure 11.6 shows extracts of a program that declares a cursor named finalists that refers to all the year 3 students in the STUDENTS table. The cursor is declared and opened in the usual way. The do..while loop near the end of the program contains a DELETE statement which deletes all the year 3 students from STUDENTS. Here's how it works. When the loop is executed for the first time, The FETCH statement causes the cursor to point to the first row of the results table ie. to the first year 3 student's row. The actual field values of this row are retrieved into the host language variables a, b, c, d, e and f. The DELETE statement:

```
exec sql delete from students
    where current of finalists ;
```

tells the DBMS to delete the row which the cursor is currently pointing to. In this case, this is the first year 3 student's row.

When the loop is repeated, the FETCH command causes the cursor to point to the next year 2 student's row and this too is deleted by the DELETE with WHERE CURRENT OF clause. When the last has been deleted, the DBMS returns a code to the program which tells it to exit the loop and jump to the appropriate program section.

We have illustrated the case of updating data via cursors by using the DELETE statement. You can also use UPDATE in exactly the same way to modify the

```
main ( ) *
{
    .
    .
    .
    /* Variable declaration section */
    .
    .
    .

    /* Declare cursor */
    exec sql declare finalists cursor for
        select * from students
                    where year = 3 ;

    /* Open cursor and run the query*/
    exec sql open finalists ;

            .
            .
            .
/* Any other processing */

            .
            .
    /* Delete all year 3 students */
    do {
        exec sql fetch finalists into :a, :b, :c, :d, :e, :f ;
        exec sql delete from students
            where current of finalists ;
    } while(1)
            .
            .
    /* Any other processing */
            .
            .
            .

    /* Error handling routines */
}
```

Figure 11.6   Use of the DELETE with WHERE CURRENT OF clause

value of rows on the same principle. To be updatable (by either DELETE or UPDATE), the cursor must satisfy the same criteria as an updatable view.

11.6 SQL Statements That Fail: Error Handling

You've seen in the programs of Figures 11.1 and 11.4 that we have used the error and warning handling statements without much explanation of how they operate.

The SQL error handling allows you to identify run-time errors and warnings produced by the DBMS and to act on them. Run-time errors are those that result from running the program, for example if an embedded SQL statement refers to a table which does not exist, then the DBMS will signal a run-time error. The error handling routines provided by SQL only apply to errors and warnings produced by the DBMS. They do not deal with the run-time errors generated through the host language.

The DBMS reports all errors and warnings to the program through a structure called the SQL Communications Area or SQLCA. The first line of the program of Figure 11.1 is:

```
exec sql include sqlca;
```

This tells the precompiler that we will be using SQL's error handling features later in the program. Whenever an SQL command is executed, the DBMS sets the value of a variable, called sqlcode, in the sqlca structure to indicate that the command was successfully executed (sqlcode set to zero), that the command failed as a result of an error (sqlcode set to a negative value) or that the command was executed but generated a warning (sqlcode set to a positive value).

You tell SQL how to deal with errors and warnings by the WHENEVER statement. There are three versions of WHENEVER which correspond to the "serious error", "warning" and "row not found" possible results of executing an SQL command. For example, in the program of Figure 11.1:

```
exec sql whenever sqlerror goto error_handler;
exec sql whenever not found goto no_number;
```

The first statement tells the precompiler to generate code which will cause the program to jump to the part of the program labelled as "error_handler". The second statement causes the program to jump to the "no_number" label if any SQL command returns a row not found warning. Note that the "row not found" is a particular type of warning which is specified by sqlca.sqlcode having a value of 100 (positive indicates a warning and 100 indicates the nature of the warning i.e. "row not found"). The third WHENEVER statement is:

```
whenever sqlwarning goto wrng_hdlr
```

We have not used it in our programs, but it will cause the program to jump to the label "wrng_hdlr" whenever an SQL command generates a warning (sqlca.sqlcode has a positive value). If we had not used the WHENEVER statements in the program of Figure 11.4, the do..while(1) loop would have repeated forever. The fact that the FETCH statement in this loop generates a warning when the last row has been retrieved causes the program flow to jump from the loop to the "no_more_rows" label.

SQL Tips

> The ANSI/ISO standard specifies the NOT FOUND warning, but does not specifiy the particular value that must be returned.

If no WHENEVER statements are defined, the default condition is to ignore the warnings and errors generated by the SQL commands. This is what will happen to the warnings generated in the programs of Figure 11.1 and 11.4 because we have not used the WHENEVER SQLWARNING commands. We could have explicitly stated this by using CONTINUE. For example, to explicitly tell the program to ignore warnings, we could add the line:

```
exec sql whenever sqlwarning continue;
```

It is good programming practice to add this line instead of leaving out the WHENEVER SQLWARNING condition altogether because it clearly indicates that you wish the warnings to be ignored and not that you've simply forgotten to add it.

SQL Tips

> The SQLCODE variable, used for reporting errors and warnings is supported by the ANSI/ISO standard and is implemented by all commercial embedded SQL products

11.7 Dealing With NULL Values: Indicator Variables

As we have seen, NULLs are special markers that are used by SQL whenever a value in a field is not known. The concept of NULL markers is not used in any common programming language. Because of this, host language variables cannot directly be assigned NULL values.

SQL Tips

> The use of indicator variables in retrieving NULL values is not specified by the ANSI/ISO standard

In order to accommodate NULLs, the host language uses indicator variables. These are integer type variables that are used in conjunction with regular host language variables and indicate if the value in the host language variable is a NULL or not. For example, if the FETCH statement in the program of Figure 11.4 could retrieve a NULL value for the HEAD column in the DEPARTMENTS table, then we must allow for this by using an indicator variable with the d_head host language variable. The modified FETCH would be:

```
exec sql fetch dptcurs
        into :d_no, :d_name, :d_headINDICATOR:n_hd, :budget ;
```

The variable, n_hd, is used as an indicator variable. It must first be declared just as any other host language variable. The keyword INDICATOR tells us that n_hd is used to indicate if d_head is set to a NULL value by the FETCH. If a NULL value is produced for d_head, the indicator variable, n_hd will be set to a negative number. The program can check the value of n_hd and carry out the appropriate actions (such as display a message "No head assigned" in the column) if a NULL is detected.

Indicator variables can also be used to assign NULL values to SQL columns. The indicator variable must first be set to a negative value and then appended to the host language variable in the INSERT or UPDATE statement. For example, to set the BUDGET value in the DEPARTMENTS table to NULL, the programmatic SQL sequence of commands is:

```
n_bdg = -1;
exec sql insert into departments
    values (:d_no, :d_name, :d_head, :budget:n_bdg, :p_budget);
```

The n_bdg variable is assigned a value of -1 and is then used in the SQL statement as an indicator variable. The negative value tells the DBMS to insert a NULL value for the BUDGET column regardless of the current value of the budget host variable.

11.8 A Library of SQL Functions: The SQL API

Some commercial SQL systems take a different approach to programmatic SQL. Rather than using embedded SQL, products such as SQL Server, SQLBase and Oracle (which also offers embedded SQL) use the SQL application program interface. The host language sees the application program interface (API) as just another library of prepackaged routines and functions.

The names and syntax of the API functions vary from one DBMS to another, and from one host language to another but most SQL APIs follow the same general principles:

–   They provide an API function to make a logical connection to the SQL DBMS.

–   They provide a function to send an SQL command, in the form of a text string, to the DBMS.

–   The API provides functions to check the status of the DBMS and to handle any errors.

–   The API provides the host language functions to DECLARE, OPEN, FETCH and CLOSE cursors.

–   At the end of the program, the API provides a function to enable the program to drop the logical connection to the DBMS.

Most commercial SQL implementations provide many more API functions then the basic ones described. Microsoft SQL Server's API for instance consists of over a hundred different functions. A typical SQL program might only use about a dozen of them.

Unlike the embedded SQL statements used in mainframe languages, which are stored as an application plan, API calls are parsed, validated, optimised and executed all at run time, rather like interactive SQL statements.

SQL Tips

Oracle's primary method of programmatic SQL is embedded SQL but it also supports the API method through the Oracle Call Interface.

Having to parse, validate and optimise SQL statements at run time results in slower program execution but many commercial SQL implementations incorporate additional features that help in speeding up program execution. SQL Server for example uses the concept of stored procedures. These are a sequence of SQL commands that are given a name and stored in the database already parsed, validated and optimised. At run time, the program makes API calls to execute stored procedures rather than complex sequences of SQL commands.

Appendix A
The ANSI/ISO standard data types

The ANSI/ISO standard only specifies eight data types that can be used to represent the data stored in tables.

1. CHARACTER(len) or CHAR(len) — Fixed length character string. The len argument refers to the maximum length of the string. All character type values must be enclosed in single quotes ('...').

2. INTEGER or INT — Integer types are whole numbers (without a decimal point). INT types are frequently used as row identifying columns eg. SUB_NO, LECT_NO, EXAM_NO etc, usually a 32-bit signed integer.

3. SMALLINT — Same as INTEGER type, but used for smaller numbers. Usually a 16-bit signed integer.

4. DECIMAL(prec, scale) or DEC(prec, scale) — Used to represent real numbers (i.e. with a decimal point). The precision argument specifies how many significant digits the number is to have. The scale argument is optional and specifies how many digits are to appear after the decimal point.

5. NUMERIC(prec, scale) — The same as DECIMAL type, except that the precision argument specifies the maximum number of digits that may be used.

6. FLOAT(prec) — Floating point numbers in scientific (base 10) notation. The precision argument specifies the minimum precision of the data.

7. REAL — Same as float, but no minimum precision is specified.

8. DOUBLE PRECISION or DOUBLE — Same as REAL, but the implementation-defined precision is greater than that for REALs.

181

Appendix B
The Sample University
Administration Database

The university administration database is used in most of the examples in this book. The database consists of five tables:

1. The STUDENTS table, which holds details of the students in the university.

2. The LECTURERS table, which holds details of the teaching staff at the university.

3. The SUBJECTS table, which holds details of the subjects that are available.

4. The EXAMS table, which holds details of all the exams taken by the students.

5. The DEPARTMENTS table, which holds details of the various departments (faculties).

The SQL statement used to create each table is shown below:

```
CREATE TABLE      (SURNAME        CHAR(15) NOT NULL,
STUDENTS          FIRST_NAME      CHAR(15),
                  D_O_B           DATE,
                  STUDENT_NO      INTEGER NOT NULL UNIQUE,
                  DEPT_NO         INTEGER,
                  YEAR            DECIMAL(2) );


CREATE TABLE      (SURNAME              CHAR(15) NOT NULL,
LECTURERS         INITL                CHAR(4),
                  LECT_NO              INTEGER NOT NULL,
                  DEPT_NO              INTEGER,
                  SUB_NO               INTEGER,
                  GRADE                CHAR(1),
                  PAY                  DECIMAL(6),
                  JOINED               DATE
                  UNIQUE (SURNAME,     LECT_NO) );
```

```
CREATE TABLE      (SUB_NO         INTEGER  NOT NULL UNIQUE,
SUBJECTS          SUB_NAME        CHAR(20),
                  DEPT_NO         INTEGER,
                  CREDITS         NUMERIC(2),
                  PASS            NUMERIC(2) );


CREATE TABLE      (SUB_NO         INTEGER NOT NULL,
EXAMS             STUDENT_NO      INTEGER NOT NULL,
                  MARK            DECIMAL(3),
                  DATE_TAKEN      DATE );


CREATE TABLE      (DEPT_NO            INTEGER NOT NULL,
DEPARTMENTS       DEPT_NAME          CHAR(20),
                  HEAD               INTEGER,
                  BUDGET             DECIMAL(10),
                  P_BUDGET           DECIMAL(10),
                  UNIQUE (DEPT_NO)  );
```

The contents of the university database tables are shown in Figure B.1.

SURNAME	FIRST_NAME	D_O_B	STUDENT_NO	DEPT_NO	YEAR
Duke	Fitzroy	11-26-1970	1	4	2
Al-Essawy	Zaid M A	11-26-1970	2	4	2
Ayton	Phil J M A	07-13-1967	3	3	1
Patel	Mahesh	12-07-1970	4	2	1
Jones	Gareth P Y	01-24-1970	5	2	1
Scott	Gavin T J	02-20-1971	6	2	2
Baker	Abu-Mia	03-13-1971	7	4	1
Brown	Joseph P A	04-19-1970	8	3	3
Monkhouse	Robert Jones	05-23-1967	9	1	1
Grimm	Hans Johan	06-21-1971	10	2	1
Gyver	Sue L J V	07-30-1968	11	4	2
Hung-Sun	Jimmy Lau	08-1-1969	12	1	3
Middleton	Jane P	09-14-1971	13	1	3
Mulla	Farook F U	10-24-1968	14	3	2
Layton	Hugh	11-16-1971	15	5	1
Wickes	Wendy Y Y W	12-05-1969	16	1	1

THE STUDENTS TABLE

Figure B.1   continued overleaf

SURNAME	INITL	LECT_NO	DEPT_NO	SUB_N	GRADE	PAY	JOINED
Jones	R A	1	1	2	E	24000	03-25-1990
Scrivens	T R	2	3	1	D	31800	09-30-1986
Nizamuddin	WM	3	3	4	A	86790	05-26-1969
Campbell	J G	4	5	3	C	43570	02-23-1980
Ramanujan	S	5	4	5	C	40900	01-01-1985
Finley	G Y	6	4	5	D	34210	03-28-1960

THE LECTURERS TABLE

SUB_NO	SUB_NAME	DEPT_NO	CREDITS	PASS
1	Mathematics	1	2	65
2	English Lit	2	1	60
3	Engineering Drwg	1	1	71
4	Basic Accounts	3	1	67
5	Industrial Law	4	2	52
6	Organic Chemistry	5	3	57
7	Physiology	6	3	78
8	Anatomy	6	1	74
9	Electronics	1	3	71
10	Marketing	3	2	56

THE SUBJECTS TABLE

SUB_NO	STUDENT_NO	MARK	DATE_TAKEN
1	1	76	05-23-1984
9	1	42	05-20-1984
3	1	67	05-15-1984
2	2	52	06-05-1984
2	3	89	06-08-1984
2	3	51	05-11-1984
4	4	34	05-11-1984
10	4	49	06-26-1984
5	5	62	05-03-1984
5	6	70	05-17-1984
5	7	36	05-23-1984
5	8	52	05-20-1984
6	9	67	05-15-1984
6	10	82	06-05-1984
6	11	73	06-08-1984
7	12	27	05-11-1984
8	12	56	05-11-1984
8	13	67	06-26-1984
7	13	63	05-03-1984

THE EXAMS TABLE

Figure B.1   continued overleaf

DEPT–NO	DEPT–NAME	HEAD	BUDGET	P_BUDGET
1	Engineering	59	5780000	6200000
2	Arts & Humanities	23	753000	643000
3	Management Studies	3	2510000	1220000
4	Industrial Law	12	78000	210000
5	Physical Sciences	18	4680000	4250000
6	Medicine	67	6895000	6932000

THE DEPARTMENTS TABLE

Figure B.I   The University Administration Database

Index